CURAÇAO
TRAVEL GUIDE
2023

**A Comprehensive Guide To Exploring the Fascinating History, Hidden Gems, and Natural Wonders of Curaçao.
A Guide To The Best Beach Vacation For First Timers.**

NATHAN A. RIVERS

Table of Contents

Top Sights and Landmarks
Willemstad
Queen Emma Bridge
Hato Caves
Fort Amsterdam

National Parks and Wildlife Reserves
Christoffel National Park
Shete Boka National Park
Sea Aquarium
Washington-Slagbaai National Park
Jan Thiel Lagoon and Wetlands
Flamingo Sanctuary
Curaçao Ostrich Farm

Top Beaches in Curaçao
Cas Abao Beach
Grote Knip Beach
Playa Porto Marie
Blue Bay Beach
Jan Thiel Beach
Kleine Knip Beach
Playa Kalki
Mambo Beach
Klein Curaçao

CHAPTER 1: WELCOME TO CURAÇAO

Curaçao is a tiny island situated in the southern Caribbean Sea, right off the coast of Venezuela. The island is a component nation of the Kingdom of the Netherlands and is noted for its lively culture, magnificent natural beauty, and year-round pleasant weather.

Curaçao has a rich history, with influences from the Dutch, Spanish, African, and Caribbean civilizations. This combination of cultures is visible in the island's distinctive architecture, gastronomy, music, and art.

The island is a popular holiday destination, attractinging people from all over the globe who come to enjoy its sandy beaches, crystal-clear seas, and numerous activities. Whether you're interested in relaxing on the beach, discovering the island's natural beauties, or immersing yourself in the local culture, Curaçao offers something for everyone.

One of the island's most recognized attractions is its capital city, Willemstad, which is a UNESCO World Heritage site. The city is famed for its colorful colonial-style buildings and scenic shoreline, where you can watch boats float past while you sip on a delicious beverage.

Curaçao's natural treasures are equally amazing. The island is home to numerous national parks and wildlife reserves, where you can walk across harsh terrain, observe rare species, and discover amazing geological formations.

Of course, no vacation to Curaçao is complete without eating the native food. The island's gastronomy is a combination of African, Dutch, Spanish, and Caribbean influences, resulting in a unique and wonderful balance of tastes. Be sure to taste some of the local delicacies, such as keshi yena (stuffed cheese), funchi (a cornmeal dish), and iguana soup.

We hope that our travel guide will help you explore everything that Curaçao has to offer. Whether you're a first-time visitor or a seasoned traveler, we know that you'll fall in love with the island's breathtaking beauty, warm people, and rich culture. So pack your bags, grab your sunscreen, and get ready to discover the hidden beauties of Curaçao!

Brief History of Curaçao

Curaçao has a rich and intriguing history that spans over 5,000 years. The island has been inhabited by many indigenous cultures, including the Arawak and the Caquetio Indians, who left behind evidence of their existence in the form of petroglyphs and other artifacts.

In 1499, the Spanish adventurer Alonso de Ojeda became the first European to reach Curaçao. The island was first claimed for Spain but was subsequently captured by the Dutch in 1634. The Dutch constructed a trade port on the island and started farming products like tobacco, sugar, and indigo.

The Dutch West India Company acquired possession of Curaçao in 1634 and built a colony on the island. The firm utilized Curaçao as a headquarters for its activities throughout the Caribbean and the Americas, and the island rapidly became an important hub of commerce.

Throughout the 17th and 18th centuries, Curaçao developed as a trade center, with items such as slaves, sugar, and rum coming through its ports. The island's main city, Willemstad, blossomed into a thriving commercial hub, with merchants from all over the globe flocking to conduct business there.

In the 19th century, Curaçao's economy evolved away from agriculture and towards oil refining. The island's refinery, which was founded in 1915, became one of the biggest in the world and provided enormous income to the island.

During World War II, Curaçao played an essential part in the Allied war effort. The island's oil refinery was a critical supply of fuel for the Allies, and the island was extensively fortified to defend it from German invasion.

In 1954, Curaçao became an independent republic within the Kingdom of the Netherlands. The island continued to grow during the 20th century, with its economy expanding to include tourism, financial services, and other sectors.

Today, Curaçao is a dynamic and diversified island that cherishes its rich history and customs. The island's colorful colonial-style buildings, museums, and historic sites give a glimpse into its history, while its blooming arts and cultural sector highlights the ingenuity and brilliance of its inhabitants.

Geography and Climate of Curaçao

Curaçao is a little island located in the southern Caribbean Sea, roughly north of Venezuela. It is one of the ABC islands, along with Aruba and Bonaire, and is part of the Lesser Antilles collection of islands. The island is fairly flat, with its highest point reaching barely over 370 meters (1,200 feet) above sea level.

Curaçao has a semi-arid climate, with year-round high temperatures and limited rainfall. The island receives an average of 22 inches (560 mm) of rainfall per year, with the rainy season coming between October and January. The island is positioned outside of the hurricane belt, so it is not commonly hit by tropical storms or hurricanes.

The average temperature of Curaçao is around 27°C (81°F), with slight fluctuations throughout the year. The island receives trade breezes that produce a cool breeze, making the atmosphere acceptable even during the hottest months.

Curaçao is famous for its magnificent beaches and crystal-clear oceans, with an average water temperature of around 27°C (81°F). The island is surrounded by coral reefs, which make it a popular place for snorkeling and diving.

Despite its relatively small size, Curaçao features a variegated landscape, with high cliffs, cactus farms, and hard terrain in certain places, while others are covered in lush flora. The island is home to various national parks and wildlife reserves, including Christoffel National Park, which provides guests the ability to hike over hard terrain and witness endangered animals.

The terrain and temperature of Curaçao make it a delightful and unique site for tourists looking to experience a tropical paradise with many opportunities for outdoor activities and discoveries.

Curaçao's Neighborhood

Curaçao is split into numerous communities, each with its own character and charm. Whether you're hunting for a lively urban hub or a calm beach refuge, Curaçao has lots to offer.

One of the most popular sites in Curaçao is the ancient city center of **Willemstad**. Known for its colorful colonial buildings and vibrant streets, Willemstad is a UNESCO World Heritage Site that is home to various restaurants, cafés, and stores. Visitors may visit the iconic floating market, meander along the waterfront promenade, and learn about the island's history at the different museums and landmarks in the neighborhood.

Another noteworthy area in Curaçao is the wealthy residential community of **Jan Thiel**. Located in the eastern section of the island, Jan Thiel is home to various luxury resorts and villas, as well as a selection of boutiques and restaurants. The region is famous for its gorgeous beaches, notably the legendary Jan Thiel Beach, which gives plenty of options for swimming, sunbathing, and water sports.

For those seeking a more laid-back atmosphere, the region of **Westpunt** is a wonderful option. Located on the western tip of the island, Westpunt is famous for its rugged shoreline, calm beaches, and outstanding natural beauty. Visitors may explore the rugged terrain of Christoffel National Park, swim or dive at Playa Knip, or simply rest and enjoy the peace and quiet of this magnificent region.

Other significant areas in Curaçao include the vibrant commercial hub of **Punda**, the attractive fishing village of **Lagun**, and the calm seaside enclave of **Sint Willibrordus**. Each district has its own individual attractions and experiences, making Curaçao a diverse and exciting destination for tourists from all over the world.

The People and Culture of Curaçao

The people and culture of Curaçao are a blend of different influences, reflecting the island's rich history and unique location in the Caribbean Sea. The population of Curaçao is made up of a mix of many nations, including Afro-Caribbeans, Dutch, Latin Americans, and more.

Curaçao's culture is often regarded as a blend of African, European, and Caribbean components. The island's music, art, and cuisine all reflect this unusual blend of cultures. Traditional music on the island is mostly influenced by African rhythms and is generally accompanied by the tambu, a local drum. Other famous genres of music on the island include salsa, merengue, and zouk.

Curaçao's gastronomy is also a reflection of its diverse cultural influences. The island is known for its seafood, particularly fresh fish, shrimp, and lobster. Other popular dishes include **stoba**, a form of stew prepared with beef or goat meat, and **keshi yena,** a meal created with cheese, meat, and spices. Local drinks include the legendary Blue Curaçao liqueur, created from the peel of the island's laraha fruit, as well as awa di lamunchi, a delectable limeade.

In addition to its music and cuisine, Curaçao is also famous for its burgeoning art scene. The island is home to several creative artists and artisans who make a variety of works in diverse styles and materials. Visitors may visit galleries and art studios around the island, or attend one of the various cultural events and festivals that take place throughout the year.

With its various influences and rich cultural past, Curaçao is a lively and exciting destination for tourists from all over the world.

Language in Curaçao

The official language of Curaçao is Dutch, because the island is a component country of the

Kingdom of the Netherlands. However, the mass of the population speaks Papiamento, a Creole language that has emerged over centuries of contact between different ethnic groups on the island, including African slaves, Dutch immigrants, and indigenous people.

Papiamento is a unique blend of African, Portuguese, Spanish, Dutch, and Arawak Indian languages, and is spoken by the majority of the inhabitants of Curaçao. It is recognized as an official language alongside Dutch, and is also largely spoken in neighboring Aruba and Bonaire.

English and Spanish are also extensively spoken in Curaçao, mainly in tourist areas and among the island's expat community. Visitors to the island will find that many individuals are able to communicate in several languages, making it simpler to get around and engage with the local community.

In addition to its official and frequently spoken languages, Curaçao is also home to a spectrum of other languages spoken by smaller parts of the population. These include Portuguese, Chinese, and Hindi, reflecting the island's varied cultural influences and immigration populations.

Travelers to Curaçao will realize that language is not a barrier to communication or interaction with the local people. With a range of languages spoken and a warm and welcoming atmosphere, guests will feel completely at home in this wonderful Caribbean resort.

Religion in Curaçao

Religion in Curaçao is diversified and reflects the island's ethnic background. The predominant religion on the island is Roman Catholicism, which was founded during the period of Dutch colonial administration. Today, over half of the population identifies as Catholic, and there are various Catholic churches and religious organizations across the island.

In addition to Catholicism, there are also large Protestant and Evangelical Christian groups in Curaçao. These include the Dutch Reformed Church, the Seventh-Day Adventist Church, and the Jehovah's Witnesses. The island is also home to several Jewish synagogues, illustrating the history of a Jewish community in Curaçao stretching back to the 17th century.

Aside from these more important religions, there are also smaller religious organizations in Curaçao, including the Baha'i faith, Islam, and Buddhism. The island's variegated religious environment reflects the global background of its residents, who have brought their faiths and traditions with them from around the world.

Despite the different religious landscape, Curaçao is recognized for its religious harmony and tolerance. The island's communities of many faiths often join together to celebrate religious holidays and festivals, and there is a spirit of mutual tolerance and cooperation among different religious groups.

Religion plays a large role in the cultural character of Curaçao, and visitors to the island will find a selection of religious monuments and organizations to explore. Whether one is interested in seeing historic churches, synagogues, or mosques, or simply experiencing the rich and active religious culture of the island, Curaçao gives a unique and interesting religious environment to explore.

CHAPTER 2: WHY YOU SHOULD VISIT CURAÇAO

Curaçao is more than simply a tropical paradise. It's a dynamic mixing pot of cultures, a kaleidoscope of hues, and a destination for adventure seekers and leisure aficionados alike. Come experience the charm of Curaçao, and you'll understand why it's an island that really has it all. Here are just a few reasons why you should consider visiting Curaçao:

Beautiful Beaches

Curaçao is famous for its stunning, calm beaches with crystal-clear oceans and silky white sand. With over 35 beaches to select from, holidaymakers may enjoy everything from calm, shallow bays to harsh, rocky coves.

Rich Culture and History

Curaçao has a diversified cultural background that is visible in its architecture, gastronomy, and arts. From the old capital city of Willemstad with its colorful Dutch colonial architecture, to the island's museums and art galleries, there is plenty to see and learn about in Curaçao.

Outdoor Activities:

With its temperate climate and stunning natural environment, Curaçao is a dream for outdoor enthusiasts. Visitors may enjoy anything from snorkeling and scuba diving to hiking and mountain biking.

Wonderful Food:

Curaçao has a unique blend of African, European, and Latin American influences in its cuisine, resulting in a fascinating and diverse gastronomic scene. Visitors may try local dishes such as stobá (a hearty stew), funchi (a kind of polenta), and pastechi (savory turnovers).

Festivals and Events:

Curaçao is famous for its interesting festivals and events, including the colorful Carnival celebration in February and the biennial Curaçao North Sea Jazz Festival. These events provide tourists a chance to experience the vibrant culture and hospitality of the island.

Curaçao gives a unique and delightful Caribbean experience that is perfect for anyone seeking adventure, pleasure, and cultural enrichment. With its magnificent natural surroundings, rich history and culture, and friendly and hospitable people, Curaçao is a must-visit destination for those seeking a really unique travel experience.

My Vacation in Curaçao

I was going through my social media account one day when a post from a buddy grabbed my attention. She had recently returned from a visit in Curaçao, and her pictures of the crystal-clear seas and gorgeous beaches were just amazing. As a person who loves adventure and the outdoors, I had heard a lot about this Caribbean paradise, and I couldn't wait to see it for myself.

I vividly recall the joy I had as I boarded my plane to Curaçao. As the plane arrived and I walked out into the balmy Caribbean air, I knew I was in for the adventure of a lifetime.

The first thing I did was check into my hotel, situated on the lovely Mambo Beach. The view from my balcony was just magnificent - the blue lake, white beach, and palm palms dancing in the mild air. I spent the rest of the day lying on the beach, drinking a refreshing drink, and watching the waves sweep in.

The following day, I was ready to start touring the island. My first destination was the magnificent Queen Emma Bridge, which unites the two sections of Willemstad. I walked over the bridge and found myself in the middle of the historic area, surrounded by beautiful colonial-style buildings, attractive shops, and great restaurants.

One of the pleasures of my vacation was seeing the Curaçao Sea Aquarium. As a fan of marine life, I was in ecstasy as I saw all types of exotic water animals up close - from sharks and stingrays to sea turtles and jellyfish. I also got to swim with dolphins, which was a wonderful experience.

Another highlight was seeing the Hato Caves, a beautiful natural creation with stalactites and stalagmites that stole my breath away. I also visited Fort Amsterdam, a historic monument with a rich history that gave an insight into Curaçao's past.

The island have a total of 38 beaches, each with its own special appeal. I visited a number of them during my trip and was astounded by the crystal blue water and beautiful, white sand. I especially loved visiting Playa Kenepa Grandi, Playa Porto Mari, Playa Cas Abao and Playa Kalki, where I took a diving lesson.

I arrived at the diving facility early in the morning, excited to start my journey. The diving instructor greeted me and gave me a lecture on what to anticipate. I was a bit nervous, but also enthusiastic to explore the underwater environment.

We boarded a boat to the diving location, which was approximately 30 minutes out from the beach. As soon as we reached the area, I could see the crystal-clear water and the vivid coral reefs that surrounding us. I put on my diving gear and took a big breath as I dived into the sea.

As I plunged lower into the water, I discovered a whole new universe. The colors were more vibrant than anything I had ever seen, and the marine life was diversified and prolific. Schools of beautiful fish swam around me, and I even spotted a sea turtle gently swimming past. The sense of weightlessness was liberating, and I felt at peace as I swam through the sea. It was a great sensation. I spent the day diving, and each dive was just as wonderful as the first. As the sun began to drop, I stepped back aboard the boat, fatigued but pleased.

Of course, I couldn't leave Curaçao without eating some of the native food. I dined on exquisite seafood, fresh fruit, and cool cocktails like the island's famed blue Curaçao cocktail. I also had some of the native desserts, such as the delicious cornmeal pudding called tutu. At night, I enjoyed the busy nightlife and the great local liquor.

As a lone traveler, I always prioritize my safety, and I felt quite comfortable during my time in Curaçao. The nice residents, the presence of security officers, and the overall calm environment made me feel comfortable.

My holiday in Curaçao was an incredible experience, and I would suggest it to anybody searching for a blend of adventure, relaxation, and excellent cuisine in a safe and inviting atmosphere. I can't wait to come back again and explore more of this wonderful island.

CHAPTER 3: WHEN TO VISIT CURAÇAO

The optimal time to come to Curaçao depends on your likes and what you want to achieve on the island. Here are some elements to consider when deciding when to go to Curaçao:

Weather: Curaçao has a warm, tropical atmosphere with generally constant temperatures throughout the year. The island is positioned outside of the hurricane belt, so tourists do not need to worry about hurricane season. However, there are definite differences in weather patterns depending on the time of year.

The dry season in Curaçao stretches from **January to September**, with the driest months being **February to July**. During this summer, the island gets little to no rainfall, providing it a perfect time to visit for outdoor activities like diving, snorkeling, and hiking. The temperatures during this time range from the mid-70s to mid-80s Fahrenheit (24°C to 29°C), making it suitable for most people.

The rainy season in Curaçao stretches from **October through December**, with the wettest month being **November**. During this month, the island has more frequent rain showers and occasional thunderstorms, however the rain typically doesn't stay long. The temperatures at this time fluctuate from the mid-70s to mid-80s Fahrenheit (24°C to 29°C), making it still pleasant and comfortable.

Crowds: Curaçao is busiest during the peak season, which extends from **mid-December to mid-April.** During this season, the island could be crowded with people, and expenses for hotels and activities may be higher. If you prefer a quieter, more relaxed break, consider traveling during the low season, which stretches from **May to November**.

Activities: Curaçao boasts a range of outdoor activities, including diving, snorkeling, hiking, and sightseeing. The finest season to dive and snorkel is from **April to October**, when the water is warm and clear. If you wish to walk or explore the island's natural areas, consider traveling during the warmer, drier months of **January to April.**

Events: Curaçao organizes a variety of festivals and events throughout the year, including Carnival in **February** and the Curaçao North Sea Jazz Festival in **August**. If you intend to experience one of these events, arrange your vacation carefully.

Consider your interests and travel objectives when selecting when to visit, and be careful of the island's high and low seasons.

How to Get to Curaçao

Going to Curaçao is like entering a completely different planet. From its crystal-clear seas to its colorful culture, this island provides a genuinely unique experience. Whether you're seeking action, leisure, or a little bit of both, Curaçao offers it all. So pack your bags and get ready for a trip like no other. Here are the most common ways to get to Curaçao:

By Air: Curaçao's principal airport is Hato International Airport (CUR), which is served by multiple major airlines including American Airlines, Delta, JetBlue, United, and KLM. The airport is located around 20 minutes from the capital city of Willemstad and serves flights to and from several countries.

Here are some countries that operate direct flights to Curaçao:

United States: Several airlines operate direct flights to Curaçao from major cities in the United States, including Miami, New York, Atlanta, and Charlotte. American Airlines, Delta, JetBlue, and United are among the airlines that offer direct flights to Curaçao from the US.

Canada: Air Canada provides direct flights to Curaçao from Toronto during the winter season, while WestJet offers direct flights from Toronto and Montreal.

Netherlands: KLM is the national airline of the Netherlands and operates direct flights to Curaçao from Amsterdam.

Colombia: Avianca Airlines operates direct flights to Curaçao from Bogota.

Panama: Copa Airlines runs direct flights to Curaçao from Panama City.

Venezuela: Several airlines provide direct flights to Curaçao from Caracas, including Insel Air and Venezolana.

Caribbean Islands: Several Caribbean airlines provide direct flights to Curaçao from other Caribbean islands, including Aruba, Bonaire, St. Maarten, and Trinidad & Tobago.

By Cruise: Many cruise lines arrange stops at the port of Willemstad, which is situated in the core of the city. The port can accommodate enormous ships and offers a range of services for visitors, including restaurants, stores, and tour guides.

Here are some of the cruise lines that offer stops at the port of Willemstad:

Royal Caribbean: This cruise line has a variety of itineraries that include a stop at Willemstad, ranging from short three-night trips to longer, multi-week Caribbean cruises.

Carnival: Carnival has various unique cruise itineraries that call at Curaçao, including their Southern Caribbean and Panama Canal cruises.

Norwegian cruise Line: Norwegian Cruise Line offers a seven-day Southern Caribbean trip that includes a call at Willemstad, as well as other notable ports in the vicinity.

MSC Cruises: MSC Cruises has numerous different itineraries that stop in Curaçao, ranging from three-night mini-cruises to longer, more comprehensive Caribbean adventures.

Celebrity Cruises: Celebrity Cruises has a selection of varied itineraries that stop in Curaçao, including their Southern Caribbean, Western Caribbean, and Panama Canal cruises.

Holland America Line: Holland America Line has a selection of diverse itineraries that stop in Curaçao, ranging from their seven-night Southern Caribbean cruises to their 23-day Panama Canal & Inca Discovery trips.

By Ferry: There is currently no ferry service to Curaçao from other Caribbean islands, but there are regular ferry services between Curaçao and the neighboring island of Bonaire.

Once you arrive in Curaçao, there are different transportation alternatives accessible to aid you travel around the island. These include rental autos, taxis, buses, and private shuttles. It's also conceivable to explore the island on foot or by bicycle, especially if you're staying in the city center of Willemstad.

Curaçao Entry Requirements For Travelers

Here are some basic recommendations about visa requirements for Curaçao:

Visa

Citizens of certain nationalities do not need a visa to visit Curaçao as a tourist. They may reside in Curaçao for up to 90 days without a visa. Here are some of the countries whose nationals are exempt from visa requirements for Curaçao:

**United States, Canada, United Kingdom,
European Union, Australia, New Zealand,
Japan, South Korea, Brazil, Argentina.**

Schengen visa holders

Citizens of countries that are members of the Schengen Area, such as the European Union, may enter Curaçao without a visa if they have a valid Schengen visa.

The Schengen visa is a form of visa that lets visitors enter any of the 26 European states that are members of the Schengen Area. However, not all countries are eligible to apply for a Schengen visa. Here are some of the countries that may apply for a Schengen visa:

**United States of America, Canada, Australia,
New Zealand, Japan, South Korea, United
Arab Emirates, Israel, Brazil, Mexico,
Argentina, Chile, Singapore, Malaysia, Hong
Kong.**

Other visa requirements:

Citizens of countries not indicated above may need to seek a visa before they travel to Curaçao. The precise visa requirements will depend on the traveler's place of origin and the length and purpose of their trip.

It's vital to note that visa requirements occasionally vary, and it's always a good idea to check with the nearest embassy or consulate of Curaçao or the Dutch Kingdom to confirm the most up-to-date requirements. Additionally, travelers may be asked to produce evidence of onward travel, a return ticket, and adequate cash to cover their stay in Curaçao.

Curaçao Visa Categories

Here are the main visa categories in Curaçao:

Tourist visa: This form of visa is for persons who wish to visit Curaçao for tourist or vacation purposes. Tourist visas are generally given for up to 90 days.

Business visa: This sort of visa is for travelers who intend to visit Curaçao for business-related activities, such as attending meetings or conferences. Business visas are also given for up to 90 days.

Student visa: This sort of visa is for students who wish to study in Curaçao for an extended term. The length of the visa will depend on the duration of the academic program.

Work visa: This form of visa is for travelers who wish to work in Curaçao. To receive a work visa, the tourist must have an employment offer from a business in Curaçao and meet other qualifying requirements.

Transit visa: This sort of visa is for travelers who are going through Curaçao to another location. Transit visas are generally valid for up to 48 hours.

Visa Process and Fees

The visa process for traveling to Curaçao depends on the traveler's nationality and the cause of their visit.

For visitors from countries that do not need a visa for access to Curaçao, no visa application is necessary. However, all travelers must complete the Digital Immigration Card (DIC) online previous to arrival.

For travelers from countries that require a visa for admittance to Curaçao, the application method typically comprises submitting an application to the nearest Curaçao diplomatic facility, such as an embassy or consulate. The application may comprise a completed visa application form, passport images, documentation of trip arrangements, and other supporting paperwork as necessary.

The visa charges for Curaçao vary. It's necessary to verify with the nearest Curaçao diplomatic office for the latest visa charges and conditions.

In addition to the visa charges, travelers may also need to pay other expenditures, such as processing fees or service fees paid by the diplomatic office or visa application facility.

It's crucial to start the visa application procedure well in advance of the specified travel dates, as processing durations could vary and unanticipated delays might emerge. Travelers should also ensure that they have all the essential papers and information in order to avoid delays or complications with the visa application process.

Valid Passport

A valid passport is a prerequisite for all travelers who are traveling to visit Curaçao. The passport should be valid for at **least six months** beyond the planned date of departure from Curaçao. This suggests that if you anticipate being in Curaçao for two weeks, your passport should be valid for at least six months and two weeks.

When applying for a passport, it's vital to ensure that all the facts are exact and up-to-date. The name on the passport should match the name on the ticket, and any changes to personal data such as name or address should be updated with the passport authorities. If you have changed your name after your passport was issued, you will need to show legal papers to confirm the name change, such as a marriage certificate or a court order.

Visitors should also make sure that their passport has enough open pages for the immigration stamps that will be applied upon arrival and departure from Curaçao. If the passport is running short on pages, it may be essential to get a new passport before traveling.

It's vital to keep your passport safe during your visit to Curaçao. Visitors should keep the passport in a secure spot, such as a hotel safe, when it's not necessary. It's also a good idea to make a duplicate of the passport and keep it in a separate place from the original, in case the passport is lost or stolen.

Digital Immigration Card (DIC)

The Digital Immigration Card (DIC) is an online system that allows travelers to complete the immigration process before arriving in Curaçao. The approach is accessible for visitors who own a passport from a visa-exempt country and are going for tourism, business, or medical objectives.

To access the DIC system, travelers must complete an online form with their personal and travel information, including their flight details, passport information, and purpose of trip. The information is thereafter forwarded to the immigration authorities for review.

Once the DIC application is approved, the traveler will receive a confirmation email that includes a barcode. The barcode may be scanned upon arrival in Curaçao, allowing the traveler to circumvent the traditional immigration lineups and proceed directly to baggage claim.

Using the DIC system may help reduce the immigration process and save time once arrival in Curaçao. However, it's vital to understand that not all passengers are eligible to employ the DIC system, and some tourists may still need to follow the traditional immigration process upon arrival.

Travel Declaration Form

As a result of the COVID-19 epidemic, all travelers visiting Curaçao are obliged to file a

Travel Declaration Form ahead to arrival. This form is meant to capture critical health and contact information from travelers, in order to enable contact monitoring and public health activities.

The Travel Declaration Form may be filled online prior to departure, and should be submitted no later than 48 hours before arrival in Curaçao. The form asks travelers to provide basic personal information, as well as data about their journey itinerary and any recent travel experience. Travelers must also disclose information on their current health status, including any symptoms they may be experiencing.

Once the Travel Declaration Form is filled, travelers will obtain a confirmation email featuring a unique code, which they will need to give upon arrival in Curaçao. The confirmation email should be printed out or kept on a mobile device for fast access.

It's vital to note that neglecting to complete the Travel Declaration Form may result in delays at the airport or perhaps refusal of entrance to Curaçao. Therefore, it's encouraged that travelers complete the form well in advance of their departure date, and ensure that all information submitted is true and up-to-date.

Proof of Sufficient Funds

Proof of enough money is an essential criteria for going to Curaçao. This is because visitors must be able to prove that they have adequate money to cover their charges while in the country. This includes the cost of lodging, food, transportation, and other travel-related costs.

There are several methods to present proof of acceptable resources when entering Curaçao. One method is to show bank statements or other financial proof that reflect the traveler's ability to refund their expenditures. These documents should indicate a significant fund in the traveler's bank account or other assets that they may rapidly access.

Another possibility is to produce proof of pre-paid travel expenditures, such as hotel reservations, airfare, or excursions. This can prove that the visitor has previously made arrangements for their vacation and has the appropriate money to cover these expenditures.

It's crucial to note that the particular requirements for proof of enough money could change depending on the traveler's nationality and the purpose of their vacation. It's usually advisable to check with the nearest Curaçao diplomatic post or consulate for the latest rules and information.

Proof of Health Insurance

When visiting Curaçao, travelers are obliged to have evidence of health insurance. This is an obligatory requirement for all tourists, regardless of the duration of their stay. The health insurance coverage should cover the expense of medical care, hospitalization, and repatriation in case of a medical emergency.

The evidence of health insurance is often requested at the point of entry, such as the airport or ports. Visitors may be required to show a copy of their insurance policy or a confirmation letter from their insurance provider. The paperwork should clearly identify the name of the insured, the coverage duration, and the kind of coverage offered.

Visitors should make sure that their insurance coverage matches the criteria of the Curaçao government. The insurance should be valid for the whole time of the visit and give appropriate coverage for any possible medical bills. Travelers should also maintain a copy of their insurance policy with them at all times throughout their stay in Curaçao.

In the case that a traveler does not have evidence of health insurance, they may be asked to acquire local coverage at the point of entry. This may be costly and is best avoided by ensuring that you have proper health insurance coverage before coming to Curaçao.

Vaccination

The government of Curaçao strongly urges all travelers to be adequately vaccinated against COVID-19 before traveling to the island.

Additionally, travelers may be subject to quarantine or other public health measures if they are not vaccinated and are judged to be at risk of spreading COVID-19.

Also, it's important for travelers to be up to date on basic vaccinations, such as measles, mumps, rubella, and influenza, before coming to Curaçao or any other destination. This may help minimize the spread of common infectious diseases and protect both the traveler and the local population.

Curaçao Embassy Websites

If you are a tourist visiting Curaçao and you need help from your country's embassy, there are various embassy websites you may visit for information and services. Here are some embassy websites that may be helpful:

United States Embassy in Curaçao: https://cw.usconsulate.gov/

Canadian Embassy in Caracas, Venezuela (also serves Curaçao): https://www.canadainternational.gc.ca/venezuela/index.aspx?lang=eng

United Kingdom Embassy in Venezuela (also serves Curaçao): https://www.gov.uk/world/organisations/british-embassy-caracas

Australian High Commission in Trinidad and Tobago (also serves Curaçao):

https://trinidadandtobago.embassy.gov.au/ptsp/home.html

Embassy of the Netherlands in Caracas, Venezuela (also serves Curaçao): https://www.netherlandsandyou.nl/your-country-and-the-netherlands/venezuela/about-us/embassy-in-caracas

In addition to these websites, there are also several online travel resources that may supply you with helpful information on visiting Curaçao, including travel tips, housing choices, and things to see and do while you're there. (Check page 277)

CHAPTER 4: PRACTICAL INFORMATION YOU SHOULD KNOW AS A FIRST TIME VISITOR IN CURAÇAO

A successful trip to Curaçao begins with appropriate planning. From packing basics to studying local norms, taking the time to prepare for your trip can guarantee a stress-free and pleasurable experience.

Currency

The official currency of Curaçao is the Netherlands Antillean guilder, usually known as the florin. The currency code is ANG and the symbol is f. The guilder is divided into 100 cents.

US currencies are widely accepted in Curaçao, especially in tourist districts. However, it's vital to know that the exchange rate may not be as beneficial as it would be if you were using local money.

If you need to convert money, you may do so at banks, exchange offices, or at specified hotels. ATMs are also widely accessible over the island, and many accept international debit and credit cards. However, it's a good idea to check with your bank beforehand to see if there are any foreign transaction fees or other penalties linked with using your card abroad.

When using cash in Curaçao, it's crucial to recognize that many establishments may not accept huge banknotes, such as 100 USD bills. It's a good idea to have smaller denominations on hand for everyday purchases.

The money in Curaçao is uncomplicated to use and exchange, and there are plenty of possibilities available for individuals who need to obtain local currency. Just be cautious to check the conversion rates and any associated expenses before you make any purchases.

Language

The official language of Curaçao is Dutch, because the island is part of the Kingdom of the Netherlands. However, the majority of the population speaks Papiamentu, which is a creole language that emerged from a combination of Portuguese, Spanish, Dutch, and African languages.

English and Spanish are also frequently spoken on the island, particularly in the tourism economy. In reality, most folks in Curaçao are multilingual and are able to engage in numerous additional languages.

If you are aiming to visit Curaçao, it is important to have a basic grasp of the native language. Here are some common phrases that you might find useful:

Bon bini - Welcome
Danki - Thank you
Bon dia - Good morning

Bon tardi - Good afternoon
Bon nochi - Good evening/night
Mi non sa - I don't know
Mi ta bon - I'm good
Kiko bo ta bisa? - What are you saying?
Mi ta bai - I'm going
Ayo - Goodbye

These phrases are an excellent approach to start a discussion with locals and show your appreciation for their culture. Remember, even if you don't know the language well, making an attempt to communicate in Papiamentu may go a long way in making your time to Curaçao more pleasurable.

However, you will realize that many people in Curaçao speak English fluently, so it is easy to get by with merely English if you do not know either Dutch or Papiamentu. Additionally, many signs and eateries on the island are written in English, Dutch, and Papiamentu, so you should not have any issue finding your way around the island.

Tipping

Tipping in Curaçao is not a necessity, however it is valued in many service-oriented sectors. In general, the amount of the tip is up to the person and might vary based on the degree of service received.

In restaurants, a tip of **10-15%** is usual for excellent service. Some restaurants may add a service fee to the bill, so be careful to check before tipping. It's also worth mentioning that certain restaurants may include the tip in the final bill, particularly for bigger parties or during busy seasons.

For taxis, rounding up to the next whole number is normal practice, but you may also pay a little more if you believe the service was extraordinary.

In hotels, it's normal to offer a little tip for cleaning employees if you're staying for more than one night. The amount might vary, but a few bucks every day is typically welcomed.

It's also worth mentioning that in certain circumstances, a tip may already be included in the price of a service or product, such as for spa services or excursions. Be cautious to verify before tipping to prevent double-tipping.

Tipping in Curaçao is not mandatory, but it is a terrific opportunity to express your gratitude for exceptional service.

Safety

Curaçao is a generally safe place for travelers. However, it is always good to take measures and keep alert of your surroundings. As with any other location, there is a chance of criminality in some regions. Therefore, it is suggested to avoid lonely regions or traveling alone at night, particularly in Willemstad. The major tourist sites of Curaçao, such as Punda, Otrobanda, and the beaches, are relatively safe. However, it is always smart to take measures like storing your belongings in the hotel safe and avoiding leaving them alone on the beach.

It is also crucial to be careful of the local traditions and regulations when in Curaçao. The use of narcotics is banned in Curaçao, and it is a severe felony. Therefore, tourists should avoid using, acquiring, or transporting narcotics. Additionally, tourists are asked to be respectful of the local culture and avoid any conduct that may be deemed rude or disrespectful.

Altogether, Curaçao is a safe and inviting location for tourists, and by taking appropriate measures and being conscious of local traditions, travelers may have a memorable and delightful trip on the island.

<u>Travel Insurance</u>

Travel insurance is always a wise decision when traveling, especially while visiting Curaçao. It is a vital investment that may protect you against unforeseen events and expenses that may emerge during your holiday.

Travel insurance may cover a multitude of scenarios, such as trip cancellations or delays, medical emergencies, lost or stolen luggage, and other unplanned catastrophes. In the event of a medical emergency, travel insurance may cover the expenditures of medical treatment, including hospitalization, ambulance fees, and emergency evacuation.

When purchasing travel insurance, it is vital to clarify that the policy covers the activities you wish to undertake while in Curaçao, such as scuba diving, snorkeling, or other adventure sports.

Travel insurance is not needed for entrance into Curaçao, nevertheless it is highly recommended to ensure that you are protected in case of any unforeseen incidents. Visitors should carefully assess their travel insurance policy to ensure that they have suitable coverage for their needs and that they understand the terms and conditions of the policy.

LGBTQ + Acceptance

Curaçao is normally an open and welcoming environment for the LGBTQ+ population. Same-sex relationships are allowed and the government has taken efforts towards equality, including legalizing same-sex marriage in 2012. Curaçao's Pride celebrations have been increasing in recent years, with activities held over the island.

However, it's vital to realize that Curaçao is still a conservative nation and there may be occasional prejudice towards LGBTQ+ folks, particularly in more rural locations. It's usually a good idea to take care and be conscious of local attitudes and customs.

Medical Care in Curaçao

Curaçao has a solid medical infrastructure with different hospitals and clinics scattered over the island. The largest hospital, Hospital Nobo Otrobanda (HNO), is based in Willemstad and offers a complete array of medical services. There are also several private clinics and medical institutions that serve both locals and tourists.

In case of a medical emergency, the ambulance service is available by calling **912**. Most medical experts in Curaçao speak English, Dutch, and Spanish, making it easier for tourists to explain their medical needs.

It's crucial to recognize that medical care in Curaçao could be pricey for tourists without travel insurance. Therefore, it's very suggested to purchase travel insurance that covers medical costs before traveling to Curaçao. Visitors may also purchase medical insurance locally in Curaçao if necessary.

For non-emergency medical concerns, it's preferable to arrange an appointment with a doctor or clinic in advance. Pharmacies are widely accessible in Curaçao, and many medications that require a prescription in other countries may be acquired over the counter in Curaçao.

Emergency Contact Information

When traveling to Curaçao, it is always vital to have emergency contact information on hand. Here are some essential numbers to know:

Emergency Services: 911
In case of an emergency, phone 911 for police, ambulance, or fire services.

Medical Emergencies: 913
For medical situations, phone 913 to get in contact with an ambulance.

Tourist Police: +5999-461-3839
The Tourist Police are there to help visitors with any concerns or crises they may experience. They speak many languages, including English, Spanish, and Dutch.

Coast Guard: +5999-839-4019
For any difficulties or situations relating to the water or coast.

Roadside Assistance: +5999-199
If you require roadside assistance.

Poison Control: +5999-736-1030
If you require help with a probable poisoning or hazardous exposure.

Hospital Emergency Room: +5999-736-8000
In case of a medical emergency that needs a hospital, phone +5999-736-8000 to contact the emergency department at the St. Elisabeth Hospital in Willemstad.

It is also advisable to have the contact information for your embassy or consulate in Curaçao in case of any complications relating to your passport, visa, or legal concerns.

Health and Safety Advice For Tourist

As a visitor visiting Curaçao, it is crucial to prioritize your health and safety. Here are some ideas to bear in mind:

Stay hydrated: The environment in Curaçao is often hot and humid, so it is crucial to drink lots of water throughout the day to prevent dehydration.

Apply sunscreen: The sun in Curaçao may be fierce, so make sure to use sunscreen with a high SPF to protect your skin.

Wear proper attire: Light, breathable clothing is advised for the warm weather. However, it is necessary to dress correctly while visiting religious or cultural institutions.

Be mindful of your surroundings: As with any trip, it is crucial to be alert of your surroundings and keep your possessions safe.

Follow local laws and customs: Familiarize yourself with the laws and customs of Curaçao before you come to ensure that you do not accidentally offend anybody or breach any laws.

Use care while swimming: While the beaches of Curaçao are lovely, it is vital to practice caution when swimming. Some places may have strong currents or other risks.

Be careful while eating new foods: Curaçao has a rich culinary legacy, but if you have any food allergies or sensitivities, be sure to inquire about ingredients before trying anything new.

Seek medical treatment if necessary: If you feel sick or have an accident, seek medical assistance straight once. Be careful to bring any essential medicines or medical supplies with you.

By following these suggestions, you may assist guarantee a safe and healthy vacation to Curaçao.

Curaçao Cultural Etiquette

Curaçao, like many Caribbean islands, has a distinct cultural identity and set of norms that tourists should be aware of to ensure they are polite and courteous throughout their trip. Here are some cultural etiquette to bear in mind when visiting Curaçao:

Greetings: In Curaçao, it is normal to greet individuals with a handshake or a kiss on the cheek (the latter is more popular with women). When approaching someone for the first time, it is courteous to introduce oneself and declare your objective.

Dress Code: While Curaçao is a laid-back location, it is vital to dress correctly on specific occasions. If you want to visit a church or attend a formal function, dress conservatively. Beachwear is not acceptable outside of the beach or pool areas.

Table Manners: When eating in Curaçao, it is usual to wait for the host or hostess to request you to sit down before taking your seat. Table manners are rather casual, yet it is still necessary to be nice and considerate to your fellow diners.

Respect for Elders: In Curaçao, it is necessary to pay respect to your elders. When entering a room, it is traditional to welcome the oldest person there first. Elders are generally addressed with a title such as "Tata" (father) or "Dushi" (sweetheart).

Time: In Curaçao, timeliness is not always a high concern. It is not uncommon for individuals to be a few minutes late for appointments, so be prepared to be flexible with your schedule.

Respect for Religion: Religion has a vital part in Curaçao an society, hence it is necessary to show respect for religious rituals and traditions. If you attend a church or other religious place, dress properly and observe any rules or guidelines mentioned.

By following these cultural etiquette recommendations, you may guarantee that you have a courteous and pleasurable vacation to Curaçao.

Essentials To Pack

When planning a vacation to Curaçao, it's crucial to make sure you have everything you need to make your stay comfortable and pleasant. Here are some basics to pack:

Sunscreen: Curaçao is renowned for its sunny weather and lovely beaches, so be sure to carry a decent quality sunscreen to protect your skin from the intense Caribbean sun.

Swimwear: Don't forget to bring your swimwear, since you'll likely be spending a lot of time at the beach or pool.

Lightweight clothes: Curaçao is warm year-round, so bring lightweight clothing made of breathable fabrics like cotton or linen to keep cool and comfortable.

Comfortable walking shoes: Whether you're touring Willemstad's colorful streets or trekking through one of Curaçao's national parks, be sure to carry comfortable walking shoes.

Insect protection: Mosquitoes may be a problem in certain places of Curaçao, so take some insect repellent to prevent getting bitten.

Hat and sunglasses: Protect your face and eyes from the sun with a wide-brimmed hat and sunglasses.

Adaptor: The electrical outlets in Curaçao utilize the same kind of plug as the United States and Canada, so if you're traveling from a different region of the globe, you may need to carry an adaptor.

Travel paperwork: Make sure to include your passport, plane tickets, and any other travel documents you may require, such as your trip insurance policy.

Medications: If you use medication prescriptions, be sure to bring enough for your whole trip and stow them in your carry-on bag in case your checked baggage is lost.

Cash: While many establishments in Curaçao accept credit cards, it's always a good idea to keep some cash on hand for minor purchases or in case of emergency.

CHAPTER 5: TOURISTS DESTINATIONS AND ACTIVITIES IN CURAÇAO

Discover the hidden gems of Curaçao, from swimming in crystal clear seas to trekking through verdant landscapes, discovering colorful towns and relishing wonderful cuisines. Every minute on this exciting island is an opportunity to find a new adventure and build amazing memories.

Top Sights and Landmarks

Curaçao has a plethora of attractions and destinations for tourists to visit. Here are some of the top picks:

Willemstad

Willemstad is the capital and largest city of Curaçao. The city is famous for its colorful architecture and historic attractions that showcase the island's Dutch colonial past.

Visitors to Willemstad may visit the city's historic center, which is a UNESCO World Heritage Site, and experience the vibrant culture and Caribbean beauty of this charming city.

One of the most recognized views in Willemstad is the **Handelskade**, a gorgeous shoreline surrounded by colorful buildings that were formerly warehouses and offices for the city's trading businesses. Visitors may meander along the Handelskade and take in the wonderful views of the Sint Anna Bay, the Queen Emma Bridge, and the colorful façade of the buildings that date back to the 18th century.

Other must-visit attractions in Willemstad include the **Mikve Israel-Emanuel Synagogue,** the oldest synagogue in continuous use in the Western Hemisphere, **the Fort Amsterdam**, a historic fort that served as the headquarters of the Dutch West India Company, and the **Curaçao Maritime Museum**, which showcases the island's maritime history.

Visitors to Willemstad may also enjoy a number of activities, such as shopping at the floating market, taking a boat tour of the harbor, discovering the city's active street art culture, and tasting the local cuisine at the city's various restaurants and cafés.

Willemstad is a must-visit place for everybody traveling to Curaçao, providing a unique blend of Dutch colonial history, Caribbean culture, and spectacular natural beauty.

Queen Emma Bridge

The Queen Emma Bridge is one of the most iconic structures in Curaçao. It is a floating pedestrian bridge that unites the two sides of Willemstad - Punda and Otrobanda. This bridge is also known as the "Swinging Old Lady" and has been a key element of the island's history and culture.

The Queen Emma Bridge was constructed in 1888 and was once a toll bridge for the use of horses and carriages. It was completed in 1939 as a pedestrian-only bridge and has been serving the people of Curaçao ever since. The bridge is a vital component of the daily lives of the locals, as it gives a rapid and comfortable method to cross the St. Anna Bay.

One of the notable aspects of the Queen Emma Bridge is that it swings wide to permit enormous ships to travel across the St. Anna Bay. This is a popular sight for tourists, who can watch as the bridge swings open and closed from the adjacent restaurants and cafés.

Walking across the Queen Emma Bridge is a must-do experience for everybody visiting Curaçao. It affords magnificent views of the colorful Dutch-style buildings on both sides of the port and is a fantastic spot for shooting photos. The bridge is also a key emblem of the island's past and present, unifying the people of Curaçao with their history and culture.

Hato Caves

Hato Caves is one of the most prominent tourist destinations in Curaçao. Located on the north side of the island, near the airport, this cave system is around 200,000 years old and was generated by the erosion of coral limestone.

The cave system consists of numerous connected chambers, filled with stalactites, stalagmites, and other limestone formations. The tunnels were exploited by the Arawak Indians, the original population of the island, for shelter and religious activities.

Today, the Hato caves are open to the public, and tourists may take a guided tour to explore the caverns and learn about its history and geology. The trek takes nearly an hour and covers a distance of around 800 meters.

During the excursion, travelers will be able to see numerous chambers, including the 'bridal chamber', which is adorned with limestone formations that resemble a wedding cake. There is also a small lake inside the caves, which is home to several types of fish.

In addition to the caves, there is a café and gift shop on the grounds. The caves are sometimes employed for special events and performances, creating a unique and fascinating experience for travelers.

Fort Amsterdam

Fort Amsterdam is a historic stronghold located in Willemstad, the capital of Curaçao. The fort was created in the 17th century by the Dutch West India Company, in order to secure the island from pirates and other opponents. It served as the major headquarters of administrative and military activity for the Dutch colony of Curaçao.

Today, Fort Amsterdam is a recognized tourist site and a key landmark of the island's colonial past. Visitors may explore the grounds of the fort, which contain several historical monuments, such as the **Governor's Palace** and the **Dutch Reformed Church**. The fort also houses the offices of the governor and other government officials.

One of the attractions of a visit to Fort Amsterdam is the stunning view of Willemstad and the bay from the fort's walls. The fort's guns and other military objects also provide an insight into the island's history and the issues it encountered during the colonial era.

Fort Amsterdam is open to the public and admittance is free. Guided tours are given, and visitors may learn more about the fort's history and significance from informed local guides.

Kura Hulanda Museum

The Kura Hulanda Museum is a must-visit place for those interested in the history and culture of Curaçao. Located in the middle of Willemstad, the museum features a superbly rebuilt 18th-century merchant's mansion and provides a large collection of artifacts and exhibits that highlight the tale of the island's African and Caribbean beginnings.

The museum's permanent collection encompasses almost 1,500 objects, ranging from African masks and sculptures to slave chains and historic documents. Visitors may explore interactive exhibits that represent the island's history, from its early days as a center for the slave traffic to its participation in the abolition of slavery and its present-day culture.

One of the highlights of the Kura Hulanda Museum is its **outdoor sculpture garden**, which showcases a collection of life-sized bronze sculptures that portray many sections of African and Caribbean history and culture. There is also a **restored slave village** on the museum grounds that offers a glimpse into what life was like for enslaved people on the island.

In addition to its permanent collection, the Kura Hulanda Museum hosts temporary exhibitions and special events throughout the year. Visitors may also enjoy a meal or a drink at the museum's restaurant, which serves traditional Caribbean cuisine in a magnificent outdoor environment.

National Parks and Wildlife Reserves

Christoffel National Park

Christoffel National Park is one of the most picturesque and visited national parks on the island of Curaçao. The park is located on the west coast of the island and includes an area of 4,500 hectares. It is named after Mount Christoffel, the highest peak on the island, which stands at 375 meters above sea level.

The park is a natural oasis with different hiking paths, picnic spots, and breathtaking viewpoints. It is home to a rich mix of vegetation and wildlife, including over 200 species of birds, lizards, and other reptiles. The park also has many unique geological phenomena, such as **limestone caves** and **rock formations** that were built millions of years ago.

Visitors to the park may explore its different trails, each of which affords a unique view of the area's natural magnificence. The most popular climb is the journey up **Mount Christoffel**, which takes around two and a half hours and affords great views of the surrounding region. There are also additional shorter hikes available, including a path to the park's most recognized feature, the **Boka Tabla Cave**.

The park is open every day from **6 am to 4 pm**, and visitors are recommended to wear **comfortable clothing and sturdy shoes**. There is a modest entry fee to the park, which helps to finance its upkeep and conservation operations.

Christoffel National Park is a must-see attraction for everyone visiting Curaçao who appreciates nature, hiking, and outdoor activities.

Shete Boka National Park

Shete Boka National Park is a magnificent coastal natural reserve on the north shore of Curaçao. The park is famous for its **jagged, rocky shoreline, dramatic blowholes, and amazing sea caves.** The park is renowned for its **seven bokas**, or **inlets**, where the waves crash against the rocks with amazing intensity, causing spectacular sprays of water.

Visitors may wander along the rugged beach to view the bokas and explore the many sea caves. The park also conducts guided trips, where visitors may learn about the area's unique geology and environment, as well as the history and culture of Curaçao.

In addition to the natural charms, Shete Boka National Park is home to a variety of animals, including sea turtles, iguanas, and a diversity of bird species. The park is also an important breeding area for green and hawksbill turtles.

Visitors should bring sturdy shoes, sunscreen, and plenty of drink when visiting the park. The park is open daily from **9am to 5pm,** and admission charges are low.

Sea Aquarium

The Sea Aquarium in Curaçao is a popular location for tourists and locals alike. It is the largest aquarium in the Caribbean and is home to a broad variety of marine life, from sharks and sea turtles to dolphins and seals.

Visitors may explore the aquarium's numerous displays, which include a touch tank where you can engage with different marine animals, a coral reef exhibit displaying the beautiful and varied undersea environment, and a shark exhibit that enables visitors to observe these spectacular creatures up close.

One of the major attractions of the Sea Aquarium is its **dolphin presentations**, which take place numerous times a day. During these demonstrations, viewers may observe as the dolphins accomplish several tricks and antics, showcasing their brilliance and agility.

In addition to the exhibits and lectures, the Sea Aquarium also offers a variety of activities and experiences for tourists, including **snorkeling and diving trips, sea lion encounters, and even a chance to swim with dolphins.**

The Sea Aquarium in Curaçao is a must-visit location for everyone interested in marine life and the natural beauty of the Caribbean.

Washington-Slagbaai National Park

Washington-Slagbaai National Park is one of the most prominent natural reserves in Curaçao. Located in the northwestern side of the island, this 13,500-acre park boasts a variegated ecosystem of rocky hills, magnificent beaches, salt flats, and mangrove forests, making it an ideal destination for nature aficionados.

The park is home to a variety of plant and animal species, including **iguanas, flamingos, parakeets, and many forms of cactus**. Visitors may take a guided tour of the park to explore its magnificent walkways, hike up to the peak of **Brandaris Hill,** and enjoy spectacular views of the surrounding countryside. There are also additional peaceful beaches within the park, particularly Boka Slagbaai, which is popular among **snorkelers and divers**.

In addition to its natural magnificence, the Washington-Slagbaai National Park also boasts a substantial cultural legacy. The park comprises several historical structures, such as **Landhuis Slagbaai,** a restored 19th-century plantation house, and **the relics of a 19th-century salt mining enterprise**. Visitors may learn about the history and culture of the park through guided tours and educational programs.

The Washington-Slagbaai National Park is a must-visit place for everybody interested in witnessing the natural beauty and cultural legacy of Curaçao.

Jan Thiel Lagoon and Wetlands

Jan Thiel Lagoon and Wetlands is a gorgeous natural environment found on the eastern coast of Curaçao. The lagoon is an important breeding and feeding location for various bird species, including herons, egrets, and flamingos. In addition to the beautiful panoramas and animals, the area is also home to a variety of plant species, including mangroves and cacti.

Visitors to Jan Thiel Lagoon and Wetlands may explore the environment by foot or by boat. There are different trekking trails that snake through the marshes, offering tourists the ability to get up close to the flora and fauna of the area. Guided boat tours are also provided, giving a unique outlook on the lagoon and the surrounding surroundings.

Jan Thiel Lagoon and Wetlands is a must-visit place for nature lovers and outdoor enthusiasts visiting Curaçao. With its beautiful panoramas, diversified wildlife, and rich history, the area affords travelers a unique insight into the island's natural and cultural inheritance.

Flamingo Sanctuary

The Flamingo Sanctuary is one of the must-visit attractions in Curaçao, particularly for nature enthusiasts. Located on the west coast of the island, the sanctuary is home to hundreds of lovely flamingos. These pink birds are a sight to see and a fantastic delight for tourists visiting Curaçao.

The Flamingo Sanctuary is nestled inside the 2,000-acre salt flats of Sint Willibrordus. The salt pans itself are a spectacular sight, with enormous areas of shining salt crystals that are gathered by the locals for export. The flamingos are drawn to the region because of the saline atmosphere, which is great for the shrimp and algae that they feed on.

The greatest time to visit the Flamingo Sanctuary is between **January and August**, which is when the birds mate and lay eggs. You can see the flamingos wading across the shallow water, their long legs giving them an exquisite image as they walk smoothly over the water. You may possibly be fortunate enough to view some newborn flamingos, which are a treat to watch.

The sanctuary is a protected area, thus tourists are not permitted to enter the salt pans. However, there is a perspective from where you may observe the flamingos up close. The viewpoint is situated on the main road, and it's free to visit. You may park your vehicle and stroll up to the viewpoint, or just pull over and observe the flamingos from the road.

The Flamingo Sanctuary is an essential aspect of Curaçao's environment, and visitors are advised to respect the birds and their habitat. You should avoid making loud sounds or upsetting the flamingos in any way. This will assist to guarantee that the flamingos continue to flourish in their natural surroundings for centuries to come.

Curaçao Ostrich Farm

Curaçao Ostrich Farm is a unique and interesting location on the eastern portion of the island. The farm was formed in 1995 and is home to more than **200 ostriches, as well as other wildlife such as pot-bellied pigs, emus, and Nile crocodiles.** The farm includes over 100,000 square meters of land, making it one of the largest ostrich farms in the world.

Visitors may take guided tours of the farm to learn more about ostriches and their behavior, as well as the other animals on the farm. The tours provide a chance to watch the ostriches up close and even feed them. The farm also offers a restaurant where travelers may experience ostrich meat specialties.

Aside from the tours, there are other activities at the farm such as ostrich racing, where tourists may observe ostriches race one another in a dynamic and fascinating performance. There is also an egg hunt where visitors may seek camouflaged ostrich eggs across the estate.

The Curaçao Ostrich Farm is a lovely site to visit for families and animal aficionados. It affords a unique chance to learn about and interact with these lovely birds, as well as experience other fascinating activities.

Top Beaches in Curaçao

Cas Abao Beach

Cas Abao Beach is one of the most popular beaches in Curaçao, famous for its magnificent blue oceans, white sand beaches, and outstanding snorkeling choices. Located on the island's northern coast, it's a superb spot for a day trip or vacation.

Visitors to Cas Abao Beach may enjoy a range of water activities, including swimming, snorkeling, and scuba diving. The beach is home to a lively underwater habitat, with a variety of tropical fish and other marine animals. Snorkeling gear is available for rent on the beach, and there are also various dive stores nearby.

The beach has many services for visitors, including restrooms, showers, and changing rooms. There are also several beach bars and restaurants where guests may enjoy a cold drink or a meal.

Beyond the beach, there are different hiking trails in the adjacent hills, providing spectacular views of the coastline and the island's rocky interior. For those wishing for a more quiet experience, there are several spas and health centers nearby, giving a range of treatments and therapies.

Whether you're seeking a day of excitement or a relaxing day at the beach, Cas Abao Beach is undoubtedly worth a visit.

Grote Knip Beach

Grote Knip Beach, also known as Playa Kenepa Grandi, is a popular spot for locals and tourists alike on the island of Curaçao. This magnificent beach is located on the western side of the island, between the settlements of Lagun and Westpunt.

The beach is known for its crystal-clear oceans and gorgeous white sand, bordered by steep cliffs and lush green hills. It is a terrific spot for swimming, sunbathing, snorkeling, and diving, as the oceans are quiet and there is a wealth of marine life to uncover.

In addition to its natural beauty, Grote Knip Beach also features several comforts to make your stay more enjoyable, such as showers, restrooms, and covered spots. There are also several food vendors and beach bars around where you may enjoy local cuisine and drinks while taking in the magnificent scenery.

One of the joys of Grote Knip Beach is the stunning sunset that can be witnessed from here. The beach is known for its stunning sunsets, and many people make a point of arriving to view the sun go down over the Caribbean Sea.

If you're seeking for a pleasant and tranquil beach away from the hurry and bustle of Willemstad, Grote Knip Beach is definitely worth a visit.

Playa Porto Marie

Playa Porto Marie is one of the most popular beaches on the island of Curaçao, situated on the southwestern shore. It's recognized for its stunning blue seas, white sand beach, and colorful marine life that may be witnessed when snorkeling or diving.

Guests can engage in numerous activities such as swimming, sunbathing, snorkeling, diving, and other water activities. There's also a hiking track that goes to the neighboring salt flats, where tourists may view flamingos and other birds.

The beach is provided with chairs, umbrellas, and showers, and there are also various restaurants and pubs nearby. Visitors may rent snorkeling and diving equipment on-site, and there's also a small store offering souvenirs and beach goods.

Playa Porto Marie is readily accessible by automobile, with a huge parking area available for guests. It's also possible to access the beach via cab or bus. There's a nominal price to visit Playa Porto Marie, which goes towards maintaining the amenities and conserving the natural environment.

With its spectacular natural beauty and vast selection of activities, it's simple to understand why this beach has become a favorite with visitors and residents alike.

Blue Bay Beach

Blue Bay Beach is one of the most popular and gorgeous beaches in Curaçao. It is located on the southwestern side of the island, roughly a 20-minute drive from Willemstad. The beach is known for its crystal-clear oceans, silky white sand, and palm trees that offer shade.

There are tons of things to do at Blue Bay Beach, making it a popular spot for families and couples alike. The beach features a variety of water sports activities, including snorkeling, scuba diving, kayaking, and windsurfing. There are also several restaurants and pubs positioned immediately on the beach, serving out great local cuisine and cold drinks.

In addition to the picturesque shoreline, Blue Bay also includes a **championship golf course,** constructed by legendary golf architect William "Rocky" Roquemore. The 18-hole course affords beautiful views of the Caribbean Sea and the island's natural beauty.

Blue Bay is also home to a spectacular resort, giving a range of facilities from hotel rooms to villas. The resort offers various pools, a fitness center, tennis courts, and a spa.

Whether you're hoping to relax on the beach, explore the underwater world, or play a round of golf, Blue Bay Beach is a must-visit spot in Curaçao.

Jan Thiel Beach

Jan Thiel Beach is a lovely beach found in the eastern region of Curaçao. The beach is a popular location among tourists and locals alike, and is famous for its crystal blue oceans, fluffy white sand, and stunning palm trees that surround the shore.

In addition to its natural beauty, Jan Thiel Beach is also home to a myriad of activities that make it a popular destination for families and tourists of all ages. Visitors may enjoy a variety of aquatic sports, including snorkeling, diving, and kayaking, or simply relax on the beach with a beautiful book.

For those seeking a more active experience, Jan Thiel Beach is also home to different beach clubs and restaurants that offer a range of activities, including beach volleyball, yoga classes, and live music.

One of the most prominent features of Jan Thiel Beach is the **Jan Thiel Bay**, which is a hidden cove that offers calm waters and is perfect for swimming and snorkeling. Visitors may also explore the adjacent mangrove forests or take a boat ride to witness the picturesque coastline from the ocean.

Kleine Knip Beach

Kleine Knip Beach, often known as Little Knip Beach, is a gorgeous beach located on the northwestern coast of the island of Curaçao. The beach is a popular place for both tourists and locals alike, owing to its crystal-clear oceans and magnificent landscapes.

One of the noticeable elements of Kleine Knip Beach is its stunning surroundings. The beach is positioned at the foot of towering cliffs, which gives a wonderful backdrop for swimming, sunbathing, and relaxing on the sand. The water at Kleine Knip Beach is warm and quiet, making it a wonderful spot for swimming, snorkeling, and other water sports.

In addition to its natural beauty, Kleine Knip Beach offers a range of amenities for tourists. There are toilets and showers available, as well as a tiny snack store where travelers may grab a fast lunch or a refreshing drink. Lounge chairs and umbrellas are also available for rent, making it easy to settle in for a day of sun and fun.

For those who prefer to venture beyond the beach, there are several hiking pathways in the adjacent hills that allow panoramic views of the island and the ocean. Visitors may also rent kayaks or join a guided boat expedition to explore the adjacent caves and coves.

Caracas Bay

Caracas Bay is a delightfully picturesque bay on the south coast of Curaçao, just a short drive from Willemstad. It is famous for its clear blue oceans, white sandy beaches, and stunning views of the coastline. This is a popular spot for swimming, snorkeling, and scuba diving, with abundant marine life such as colorful fish, coral reefs, and sea turtles.

The harbor is bordered by towering cliffs, and there are many hiking trails climbing up to the hills, offering wonderful panoramic views of the surrounding country. Visitors may also rent kayaks or paddle boards to explore the area on their own, or join a boat excursion to explore the bay and nearby islands.

Caracas Bay is also home to many beach clubs and restaurants where people can relax and enjoy a meal or a drink while taking in the stunning views. **Papagayo Beach Club** is one of the most popular beach clubs, offering a colorful setting, delicious food, and cold drinks.

For those wanting for a little more action, there are many day trips and excursions available from Caracas Bay, including hikes to neighboring Klein Curaçao or the island's multiple national parks and natural reserves.

Playa Kalki

Playa Kalki is a lovely and tranquil beach situated on the western coast of Curaçao, near the municipality of Westpunt. It is one of the island's hidden beauties, situated away from the busy crowds and commercial development of some of the more prominent beaches.

The beach features crystal-clear seas, excellent for swimming, snorkeling, and scuba diving. It is a popular place among divers and snorkelers owing to the huge variety of marine life that can be observed in the waters here, including colorful fish, sea turtles, and even octopuses.

Aside from swimming and snorkeling, Playa Kalki also provides guests the ability to experience a number of water activities, including kayaking and stand-up paddleboarding. There is a tiny dive store nearby on the beach where tourists may rent equipment and sign up for diving classes or guided trips.

The beach is provided with services such as showers, bathrooms, and a beach bar that provides wonderful cuisine and beverages. For those preferring a more calm and private experience, there are also covered spots and hammocks available where guests may rest and enjoy the spectacular views.

Playa Kalki is a must-visit site for everyone wishing to enjoy the natural beauty and quiet of Curaçao.

Mambo Beach

Mambo Beach is a prominent beach attraction located in the southeastern area of Curaçao, near the capital city of Willemstad. It is a gorgeous, crescent-shaped beach that is surrounded by crystal clear water, white sand, and swaying palm palms. This beach is a popular destination for both tourists and locals alike, as it gives a comprehensive range of activities and amenities to enjoy.

One of the major attractions of Mambo Beach is the Mambo Beach promenade, which is a popular oceanfront promenade that is filled with boutiques, clubs, restaurants, and entertainment facilities. Visitors may purchase souvenirs, enjoy a refreshing drink, or taste some of the local food at one of the various cafes that dot the Boulevard.

For those wanting for a bit more adventure, there are loads of watersports and activities to select from at Mambo Beach. Visitors may hire paddle boards, kayaks, and jet skis, or join a snorkeling or diving adventure to experience the beautiful underwater habitat that surrounds the beach.

For families with children, Mambo Beach is a wonderful option, as it includes a secure and shallow swimming area, as well as a playground and other activities for kids. There is also a beach club with a pool, lounge chairs, and umbrellas, making it the perfect spot to relax and soak up the sun.

Mambo Beach is a must-visit destination in Curaçao.

Klein Curaçao

Klein Curaçao, which means "Little Curaçao" in Dutch, is a little uninhabited island located southeast of the main island of Curaçao. The island is a popular place for day visitors thanks to its spectacular white sand beaches, crystal-clear oceans, and abundant marine life.

Visitors to Klein Curaçao will enjoy swimming, snorkeling, scuba diving, sunbathing, and exploring the island's unusual nature. The island's greatest attraction is its **iconic lighthouse,** which was constructed in 1913 and towers at 20 meters tall. The lighthouse is a famous spot for capturing photos, especially after sunset.

Klein Curaçao is also home to many shipwrecks, including the ruins of a German cargo ship that was sunk during World War II. The island's waters are plentiful in marine life, making it a popular spot for divers and snorkelers. Visitors may expect to watch gorgeous tropical fish, sea turtles, and even dolphins.

The island has limited amenities, including a little beach bar and restroom facilities. Visitors are recommended to bring their own food and drinks and to carry plenty of sunscreen and water, as the island may get hot and humid.

Boat cruises to Klein Curaçao are available from several spots on the main island of Curaçao and generally include a guided tour of the island, lunch, and snorkeling equipment. The boat cruise takes roughly two hours each way and may be bumpy, so tourists should be prepared for a rather uncomfortable ride. Despite this, Klein Curaçao remains a must-see location for everybody visiting Curaçao.

Hidden Gems of Curaçao

Travel is not simply about visiting new locations, but also about uncovering the hidden jewels that are frequently buried in plain sight.

It's about venturing off the beaten road and immersing oneself in the unfamiliar. Curaçao is full of hidden gems waiting to be uncovered - all you have to do is search. Here are some of the hidden gems of Curaçao:

Boca Tabla

Boca Tabla is a natural feature found in the Shete Boka National Park on the northern coast of Curaçao. It is a magnificent cove surrounded by rugged cliffs and rocky outcrops, where the waves of the Caribbean Sea pound hard on the coast.

The phrase "Boca Tabla" means "Table Mouth" in Spanish, which is a reference to the flat, table-like rock formations that are noticed in the water. Visitors may explore the cove on foot and meander along a short footpath that snakes its way along the edge of the cliffs, affording wonderful views of the sea and the surrounding environs.

One of the primary attractions of Boca Tabla is the natural bridge that has formed in the rocks, which people may stroll over to get a closer look at the waves pounding below. Another popular activity is to take a boat tour of the cove, which enables guests to explore the rock formations and sea caves up close, as well as view a variety of aquatic animals that call the region home.

Visitors should be cautioned that the waves at Boca Tabla may be rather violent, thus it's vital to exercise care while traveling along the cliffs and natural bridge. However, for those who are prepared for a little adventure and don't mind getting a little wet, Boca Tabla is a must-see site on any visit to Curaçao.

Savonet Museum

Savonet Museum, better known as the Savonet Plantation, is a museum located in Christoffel National Park in Curaçao. The museum is situated in the midst of the historic Savonet Plantation, which was built in 1662 and was one of the largest and most productive plantations on the island.

Today, the Savonet Museum allows travelers an insight into Curaçao's colonial past and the history of the plantation. The museum features exhibits and displays that focus on the ordinary lives and work of the enslaved people who lived and worked on the plantation. Visitors may explore the recreated plantation mansion, the kitchen, the slave quarters, and the gardens.

The Savonet Museum also conducts guided tours of the plantation and its environs. Visitors may learn about the varied flora and animals that inhabit the national park, as well as the unique cultural traditions of Curaçao's Afro-Caribbean tribes.

In addition to its exhibits and visitors, the Savonet Museum also offers cultural events and activities throughout the year. These events involve music and dance performances, traditional culinary demonstrations, and lectures on crafts and traditional arts.

Saliña Sailing Club

The Saliña Sailing Club is one of the top sites to go if you're seeking for a distinctive and original experience while visiting Curaçao. The club is located in the Spanish Water, one of the most beautiful sites of the island, and offers a comprehensive range of activities for travelers to enjoy.

One of the principal activities of the Saliña Sailing Club is sailing, and visitors may charter a sailboat or take a sailing lesson from one of the skilled instructors. The waters of the Spanish Water are tranquil and translucent, making it the perfect spot for beginners to learn how to sail.

In addition to sailing, the Saliña Sailing Club also offers other water-based activities, such as kayaking and stand-up paddleboarding. Visitors may explore the spectacular beach and the mangrove woodlands that surround the Spanish Water, and get up close to the natural aquatic life.

For those who prefer to stay on land, the Saliña Sailing Club features a café and bar where travelers may enjoy a meal or a drink while taking in the amazing views. The club also offers numerous events and live music performances, making it a popular venue for locals and tourists alike.

Whether you're an accomplished sailor or just looking for a fun day out on the water, the Saliña Sailing Club is definitely worth a visit while in Curaçao.

Marshe Bieu

Marshe Bieu, generally known as the Old Market, is a notable place in Willemstad for traditional local cuisine. It's located in the core of the city and is a superb site to explore true food and culture.

The market is open for **lunch from Monday through Saturday** and is often packed with locals and tourists alike. The kiosks are maintained by local chefs and give a varied assortment of foods, including stews, soups, grilled meats, and seafood. Some of the most popular dishes include kabritu (goat stew), keshi yena (stuffed cheese), and funchi (a form of cornmeal porridge).

Aside from the food, Marshe Bieu is also famous for its colorful atmosphere. It's an excellent venue to pick up the local culture and socialize with the pleasant inhabitants. You'll regularly hear live music playing in the background and witness people dancing and enjoying themselves.

It's worth remembering that Marshe Bieu is a cash-only restaurant, so make sure to have some local money with you. Prices are normally relatively inexpensive, with most dinners costing roughly **$10-15.** The market may get fairly busy during peak hours, so it's advisable to arrive early if you want to avoid the throng.

Landhuis Dokterstuin

Landhuis Dokterstuin is a historic plantation mansion located in the northern region of Curaçao. The edifice stretches back to the 18th century and has been totally restored to its former glory, making it a popular destination for travelers visiting the island.

The property is surrounded by gorgeous gardens that are open to the public and give a tranquil refuge from the stress and bustle of everyday life. Visitors may take a leisurely tour through the gardens and observe the wide variety of tropical plants and flowers.

Inside the residence, tourists may explore the numerous rooms and learn about the history of the plantation and the island. The mansion has been transformed into a museum, reflecting the rich cultural past of Curaçao. Exhibits include antiques from the island's original people, as well as objects from the colonial era, such as furniture and pottery.

Landhuis Dokterstuin also hosts a number of cultural events throughout the year, including live music performances and art exhibitions. It is a favored place for weddings, receptions, and other special events, presenting a wonderful setting for any occasion.

Landhuis Dokterstuin is a must-visit place for everybody interested in the history and culture of Curaçao. It affords a unique insight into the island's past and is a terrific destination to spend a day visiting.

Boka Pistol

Boka Pistol is a beautiful natural feature found on the northwestern coast of Curaçao, near the town of Westpunt. This tiny inlet is termed after the terrific sounds that can be heard as the waves smash on the granite cliffs, resembling the sound of a gunshot. The water that enters the inlet generates an enormous splash that may reach up to 30 feet high, giving an awe-inspiring spectacle.

Boka Pistol is surrounded by steep cliffs and interesting rock formations that have been sculpted by the powerful waves over time. The location is a fantastic picture of the island's outstanding natural beauty, with the crystal-clear blue water and the colorful fish swimming in the port.

The finest way to see Boka Pistol is by strolling along the steep coastline, where you can experience the amazing views of the surrounding area, the sea turtles swimming in the bay, and the occasional pod of dolphins bursting out of the water. The road to Boka Pistol is well-marked and may be accessed from the adjoining parking lot. The walk is not too extensive, but it is hard and uneven, therefore it is necessary to wear sturdy shoes.

Once you arrive at Boka Pistol, you may take a refreshing swim in the crystal blue water, sunbathe on the rocky shore, or just sit back and enjoy the magnificent surroundings. It is best to visit Boka Pistol during the morning or early afternoon when the water is calmer, enabling it easier to access the entrance and swim in the bay.

Kabrietenberg

Kabrietenberg is a hill in the eastern region of Curaçao, located near the municipality of Santa Catharina. The hill is roughly 160 meters high and gives great panoramic views of the surrounding environs.

Kabrietenberg is a popular spot for hikers and wildlife lovers who prefer exploring the island's tough terrain. There are different trails that rise to the top, giving spectacular views across the island's scenery, beaches, and nearby hills. Visitors may witness different vegetation and fauna throughout the route, including cacti, wildflowers, and lizards.

One of the characteristic qualities of Kabrietenberg is its rocky terrain, which has been formed over time by the forces of nature. The hill's rugged slopes are perfect for brave travelers who adore rock climbing and bouldering. The hill is also home to several small caverns and fissures that may be explored by persons with a sense of adventure.

Kabrietenberg is located in a section of the island that is rich in history and culture. Nearby, guests may explore the hamlet of Santa Catharina, which is home to many historic attractions, including the **Santa Catharina Plantation and Landhuis Groot Santa Martha**. Visitors may learn about the island's colonial past and the role of slavery in affecting its history.

Kabrietenberg affords guests a unique opportunity to observe Curaçao's natural beauty, rich history, and diversified culture. Whether you're a hiker, rock climber, or history enthusiast, a visit to Kabrietenberg is bound to be a unique experience.

Lagun Beach

Lagun Beach is a modest, calm beach found on the west coast of Curaçao. This secluded beach is famous for its dazzling, blue oceans and abundant marine life, making it a popular site for snorkeling and scuba diving. The beach is flanked by lush green hills and rocks, creating a magnificent backdrop to the dazzling blue oceans.

The waters near Lagun Beach are home to a variety of fish species, including colorful parrotfish, sergeant majors, and blue tangs. Visitors may hire **snorkeling** equipment from the local dive store or bring their own to explore the underwater habitat. **Scuba diving** is also a popular pastime in Lagun Beach, with different dive locations positioned close offshore.

Aside from water activities, Lagun Beach is a lovely spot to simply relax and soak up the sun. The beach is fairly tranquil and uncrowded, offering it a wonderful haven away from the more popular sections of the island. There are also a few local cafes and snack bars nearby where travelers may have a bite to eat or a refreshing drink.

For those wanting to go out and explore the area, there are many trekking paths and natural wonders nearby, including the neighboring **Shete Boka National Park and Boca Tabla cave.** Overall, Lagun Beach is a must-visit site for nature enthusiasts and beach connoisseurs visiting Curaçao.

Santa Martha Bay

Santa Martha Bay is a gorgeous natural bay located on the northwest coast of Curaçao, just a short drive from the municipality of Soto. The bay is known for its crystal blue water and stunning views of the surrounding hills and rocky outcroppings. It is a popular spot for swimming, snorkeling, and diving, as well as resting on the white sand beach.

One of the most popular activities in Santa Martha Bay is **snorkeling**, thanks to the clear water and generous marine life. Visitors may swim among schools of colorful fish, marine turtles, and even small reef sharks. **Scuba diving** is also a superb choice for folks who prefer to explore deeper oceans and unearth hidden gems like tunnels and shipwrecks.

For those who prefer to stay on land, there are numerous hiking paths that provide beautiful views of the bay and surrounding landscape. The **Kabrietenberg walk** is popular with locals and tourists alike, as it affords panoramic views of the coastline and the Santa Martha Bay below.

After a day of swimming, hiking, or snorkeling, visitors may enjoy a dinner or a drink at one of the several beachfront restaurants and pubs in the neighborhood. The laid-back attitude and breathtaking natural beauty of Santa Martha Bay make it a must-visit site for everybody traveling to Curaçao.

Mushroom Forest

Mushroom Forest is a wonderful diving location situated on the northwest coast of Curaçao. The moniker "**Mushroom Forest**" derives from the distinctive mushroom-shaped coral formations that are common in the area. This dive area is excellent for intermediate and advanced divers thanks to its depth and strong currents.

The Mushroom Forest dive site is positioned in the heart of a sandy plateau, and as you dive deeper, you'll witness several tall coral pinnacles rising from the sandy bottom. The coral formations are overflowing with life, including schools of colorful fish, lobsters, moray eels, and many other aquatic species.

One of the attractions of diving in Mushroom Forest is the possibility to watch **big schools of barracudas and tarpons.** You may also spot numerous sea turtles and nurse sharks swimming among the coral formations.

The depth of the Mushroom Forest diving site runs from 40 to 100 feet, and the visibility is often high, making it a wonderful spot for underwater photography. However, thanks to the high currents in the area, it's necessary to plan your dive properly and follow the direction of an expert guide.

Mushroom Forest is a must-visit diving spot for any diver visiting Curaçao. The unusual coral formations and numerous aquatic life give for a magnificent underwater experience.

Boca Ascencion

Boca Ascencion is a lonely beach found on the northern coast of Curaçao. The beach is famous for its crystal-clear waves and is flanked by towering cliffs, which allow beautiful views of the surrounding surroundings.

To access Boca Ascencion, tourists must walk a rocky and gravel trail that leads to the shore. However, once there, guests are rewarded with a magnificent and tranquil cove, excellent for swimming, sunbathing, and snorkeling.

The beach is extremely popular with locals and tourists who are wishing to escape the congestion and spend a calm day in nature. Boca Ascencion offers a pleasant and serene ambience that is excellent for anyone seeking relaxation and serenity.

Visitors are urged to bring their own food and drinks, because there are no facilities or restaurants on the beach. Additionally, the waters of Boca Ascencion may be turbulent at times, therefore visitors are encouraged to take caution and only swim within approved zones.

Boca Ascencion is a hidden gem that is worth the effort to find. It offers a calm and lovely region, excellent for a day trip away from the hurry and bustle of the city.

Landhuis Jan Kok

Landhuis Jan Kok is a historic plantation mansion located in the northern portion of Curaçao, near the hamlet of Barber. Built in the 18th century, it was originally used for salt mining and subsequently for farming. Today, the mansion has been rebuilt and repurposed into a museum and cultural center.

The museum of Landhuis Jan Kok offers visitors an opportunity to learn about the history of Curaçao and the essential role that plantations played in the island's economy. Exhibits illustrate the different crops that were farmed on the estate, including maize, cotton, and aloe vera. There are also displays about the slaves who worked on the estate and the lives they lived.

In addition to the museum, Landhuis Jan Kok also provides attractive gardens that are open to the public. Visitors may walk about the grounds, which are rich with tropical flora, palm palms, and flowers. There is also a restaurant on site where guests may enjoy a meal or a snack while taking in the lovely scenery.

Landhuis Jan Kok is a wonderful site for those interested in history, culture, and the natural beauty of Curaçao. The museum and gardens provide a unique glimpse into the island's past, while the café gives a tranquil area to appreciate the present.

Beach Activities and Adventures

Life is great at the beach. The sun, the beach, and the sea provide a wonderful combination of leisure and adventure. A fantastic day at the beach may wash away all your troubles and leave you feeling renewed, revitalized, and ready to take on the world. Here are some of the activities you may engage in at Curaçao beautiful beaches:

Snorkeling and Scuba Diving

Curaçao is famous for its stunning beaches and crystal-clear oceans, making it a favored destination for snorkeling and scuba diving aficionados. With roughly 65 dive sites surrounding the island, guests may explore a vast range of underwater ecosystems, including coral reefs, cliffs, and wrecks.

One of the most popular diving locations in Curaçao is the **Blue Room Cave**, which is located on the west side of the island. This **underwater cave** is known for its spectacular blue light and is a favorite with snorkelers and divers alike. Other popular dive spots include **Mushroom Forest**, where divers may explore a unique collection of mushroom-shaped coral formations, and the **Tugboat Wreck**, which is home to a vast array of marine life.

For those who are new to diving or snorkeling, there are dozens of operators and dive shops that give basic training and guided tours. Many of these trips include all required equipment and transportation to and from the diving venues.

Snorkeling is also a popular hobby in Curaçao, with many of the island's beaches affording fantastic opportunities for observing colorful fish and other aquatic life. Some popular snorkeling locations include **Playa Lagun**, where travelers may swim with sea turtles, and **Cas Abao Beach**, which is home to a vast range of fish species.

Curaçao's warm waters, abundant marine life, and numerous dive locations make it a terrific destination for snorkeling and scuba diving fans of all skills.

Kayaking and Paddleboarding

Kayaking and paddleboarding are popular pastimes in Curaçao, because the calm waters around the island create the right climate for these sports. Whether you're an accomplished kayaker or paddleboarder, or a newcomer keen to try something new, there are plenty of possibilities to choose from.

One popular site for kayaking and paddleboarding is the **Jan Thiel Lagoon**, a stunning natural area that offers quiet waters and breathtaking landscapes. Here you may rent kayaks or paddle boards, or join a guided tour of the area. The lagoon is also home to a variety of bird species, making it an excellent place for birdwatching as well.

Another popular place for kayaking and paddleboarding is the **Spanish Water,** a wide lagoon that is isolated from the open sea by a short channel. Here you may paddle through mangroves and around tiny islands, and possibly stop at one of the various beaches along the way.

For those wanting for a bit more thrill, the west coast of Curaçao offers some more strenuous kayaking and paddleboarding chances. Here you may kayak through challenging terrain and find hidden coves and beaches that are unattainable by foot.

No matter where you choose to kayak or paddleboard in Curaçao, you're certain to be surrounded by magnificent terrain and crystal-clear waters, making for a wonderful experience.

Jet Skiing and Parasailing

Curaçao is not just about beaches, it's also a superb spot for adventure seekers. Among the popular water sports are jet skiing and parasailing, which allow visitors to enjoy the adrenaline of the Caribbean sea from a new perspective.

Jet skiing is a fantastic way to explore the coastline and enjoy the warm waves of Curaçao. There are many rental businesses that arrange jet ski experiences, where clients may ride solo or with a guide. The tours usually take tourists to secret beaches and other stunning spots around the island, offering a wonderful experience.

Parasailing is another popular water activity that affords stunning views of the island from above. Participants are lifted into the air by a specially manufactured parachute, which is coupled to a speedboat. As the boat rushes forward, the parachute rises higher and higher, affording guests a bird's eye view of the beach and the crystal-clear oceans below.

Both jet skiing and parasailing involve a certain degree of physical condition and are not indicated for persons who are pregnant or have medical concerns that may be worsened by the activity. However, for those who are prepared for the effort, they give a unique and fascinating opportunity to enjoy the beauty of Curaçao.

Sailing and Boating

Curaçao is a superb destination for sailing and boating fans, with crystal-clear waters and mild winds. There are different possibilities for sailing and boating activities, from sunset excursions to deep-sea fishing expeditions.

One of the most popular boating activities in Curaçao is a **day trip to Klein Curaçao**, a small desolate island lying just off the coast of the main island. Visitors may take a catamaran or sailboat to the island and spend the day snorkeling, sunbathing, and viewing the island's abandoned lighthouse.

For those seeking for a more peaceful experience, **sunset cruises** are a perfect chance to unwind while enjoying the spectacular views of the coastline. Many sailing enterprises give sunset tours with beers and snacks included, making it the perfect way to close a day in paradise.

Deep-sea fishing adventures are also given for those who like to try their luck at catching some of the huge game species that can be found in the waters around Curaçao, such as marlin, tuna, and wahoo. Most fishing expeditions include all the required equipment and the guidance of competent captains.

In addition to these choices, travelers may also charter their own sailboats, powerboats, or jet skis to explore the coastline at their own pace. With so many chances for sailing and boating, there's something for everyone in Curaçao.

Beach Volleyball and Soccer

Curaçao is a refuge for sports fans, and beach volleyball and soccer are two popular diversions that may be practiced on the island's wonderful beaches. Beach volleyball is a bright and active exercise that is great for the seaside mood. Whether you're a seasoned player or a rookie, you'll appreciate the feeling of the sand between your toes as you dive and spike your way to success. Several beaches in Curaçao are appropriate for beach volleyball and soccer, including **Mambo Beach, Jan Thiel Beach, and Playa Piskado.** These beaches give sufficient area and facilities to satisfy both solo players and organized teams. If you're a soccer fan, you'll be thrilled to know that Curaçao features multiple local leagues, and many of the island's beaches have soccer fields where you can hone your skills or challenge your friends to a game. In fact, the Curaçao Soccer Academy is situated in Willemstad and offers year-round coaching for players of all ages and talent levels. So whether you choose beach volleyball or soccer, you may enjoy these activities to the fullest in Curaçao's magnificent beach setting. With crystal-clear oceans, silky white beaches, and a warm tropical climate, there's no better area to play and soak up the sun.

Chill and Relaxation Spots in Curaçao

Curaçao is an ideal spot for folks seeking relaxation and peace. The island boasts a vast range of magnificent beaches, peaceful coves, and private locations that are perfect for hanging out and relaxing. Here are some of the finest tranquil and leisure spots in Curaçao:

Playa Lagun: This wonderful beach is surrounded by rocks and features crystal-clear waters that are perfect for swimming and snorkeling. The beach is relatively tranquil and is a wonderful spot for relaxing and soaking up the sun.

Santa Barbara Beach & Golf Resort: This wonderful resort is nestled on a peaceful beach on the east side of the island. The resort includes a spectacular infinity pool, a spa, and a number of food choices. It's the best setting to relax and admire the natural beauty of Curaçao.

Jan Thiel Beach: This famous beach is located on the east shore of the island and is noted for its clean waters and excellent sand. The beach is lined by palm trees and provides a number of beach bars and restaurants, making it a perfect spot to relax and enjoy the Caribbean vibe.

Blue Bay Beach: This magnificent beach is located on the south side of the island and is surrounded by lush vegetation. The beach has gentle waves and is perfect for swimming and snorkeling. The beach also includes a range of amenities, including sun loungers, umbrellas, and a beach bar.

Baoase Luxury Resort: This luxury resort is nestled on a private beach on the south side of the island. The resort includes stunning villas and suites, a lovely infinity pool, and a number of dining choices. It's the perfect area to relax and escape the stress and bustle of everyday life.

Grote Knip Beach: This magnificent beach is located on the west side of the island and is known for its crystal-clear waters and fine white sand. The beach is relatively tranquil and is an ideal spot for relaxing and enjoying the wonderful nature.

Mambo Beach: This bustling beach is located on the southeast coast of the island and is famous for its lively ambience and range of beach bars and cafes. The beach is an excellent spot for people watching and soaking up the Caribbean ambiance.

Boca Tabla: This natural feature is located on the west side of the island and is famous for its spectacular rock formations and pounding waves. It's a superb spot for taking in the natural beauty of Curaçao and relaxing in a calm atmosphere.

Whether you're hunting for a secluded beach or a luxurious resort, Curaçao has something for everyone.

Outdoor Activities and Adventures

Curaçao is an ideal destination for those who love outdoor adventures. Here are some outdoor activities that you can enjoy on the island:

Hiking:

Curaçao boasts a lot of wonderful hiking paths, ranging from simple to tough. Some popular paths are the **Christoffel Park trails, the Kabrietenberg route, and the Watamula trail.**

Mountain biking:

Mountain biking is a popular outdoor activity in Curaçao, allowing a unique and exciting way to explore the island's rugged nature. There are several mountain bike tracks available, ranging from beginner-level to expert, and they provide a good opportunity to get away from the crowds and admire the island's natural beauty. Some popular trails are the trails in the **Christoffel Park, the trails in Boca St. Michiel, and the trails at Sint Joris.**

Windsurfing and kitesurfing:

Curaçao is famous for its superb windsurfing and kitesurfing spots, thanks to its steady trade winds and clear oceans. Here are some of the top places for windsurfing and kitesurfing in Curaçao:

Lac Bay - Located on the southeastern tip of the island, Lac Bay is a secluded lagoon with shallow, crystal-clear waters and consistent winds. It's one of the finest windsurfing and kitesurfing locations in the Caribbean, attracting both amateurs and experts.

St. Joris Bay - St. Joris Bay is a notable area for windsurfing and kitesurfing because of its strong winds and tumultuous waves. The bay is located on the eastern side of the island, and is also an excellent spot for surfing.

Playa Kanoa - Playa Kanoa is an isolated beach on the western coast of Curaçao, boasting regular trade winds and gentle surf. It's an ideal venue for beginners and intermediate windsurfers and kitesurfers.

Playa Grandi - Playa Grandi is located on the western coast of Curaçao, and is famous for its strong winds and rough surf. It's an outstanding place for talented windsurfers and kitesurfers.

Caracas Bay - Caracas Bay is located on the southeastern side of the island, and is an ideal place for experienced windsurfers and kitesurfers. The harbor has frequent winds and powerful waves.

Just be sure to check the weather and wind conditions before going out, and always wear sufficient safety gear.

Cave exploration:

Curaçao is a little island nation that is full of surprises, and one of the greatest ways to appreciate its natural beauty is by cave exploration. The island features a variety of caves that are accessible to guests and give unique and exciting experiences.

The most popular cave in Curaçao is the **Hato Caves,** which are located near the airport. These caves were built millions of years ago and feature an astonishing assortment of stalactites, stalagmites, and other cave formations. The Hato Caves are also home to a significant population of bats, which add to the overall ambiance of the cave.

Another noteworthy cave is the **Boca Tabla Cave**, which is located on the western side of the island in the Christoffel National Park. This cave is known for its tremendous waves that crash into the cave, offering a stunning demonstration of natural force. Visitors may explore the cave and observe the remarkable rock formations that have been molded by the water over time.

For those who seek a more challenging cave exploration experience, the **Fontein Cave** is a wonderful choice. This cave is located on the western side of the island, and guests must climb to reach the entrance. Inside, guests may explore little passages and admire the amazing rock formations.

The **Blue Room Cave** is another must-see for cave fans. This cave is located on the west side of the island and is only accessible by boat or swimming. The cave is known for the brilliant blue light that illuminates the cave when the sun shines through the water. Visitors may swim in the cave's pure waters and examine the peculiar blue color.

Cave exploration in Curaçao is a fascinating and unique way to appreciate the island's natural wonders.

With so many outdoor adventures to choose from, Curaçao is an ideal destination for adventure seekers and nature lovers alike.

Guided Tours and Excursions

Exploring a new area may be a great experience, but traversing unknown territory can be scary. That's why having the assistance of an experienced professional may make all the difference in unearthing hidden treasures and generating memorable experiences. Here are a fee of your guides in Curaçao:

Jeep Safaris and ATV Tours

Curaçao is a unique and diverse island, and what better way to see it than with a Jeep safari or ATV (all-terrain vehicle) tour? These treks give a wonderful experience over the island's hard terrain and natural grandeur. Here are some of the top Jeep safari and ATV trip choices in Curaçao:

Curaçao Actief: This business offers a variety of adventures including ATV, buggy, and Jeep tours. They arrange journeys that take you to some of Curaçao's most spectacular places, including Christoffel Park, Shete Boka National Park, and the Hato Caves.

Eric's ATV Adventures: This organization organizes guided ATV rides that take you to some of Curaçao's hidden gems, such as the San Pedro Plateau and the Spanish Water Bay. They also give sunset cruises that take you to the top of a hill for a spectacular panoramic view of the island.

ABC Tours: This organization conducts Jeep safaris that bring you to some of the island's most attractive places, including the Westpunt region, where you can enjoy breathtaking views of the coast and visit the legendary Playa Kenepa beach.

Go West Diving: This organization delivers a unique ATV tour that takes you through the magnificent countryside of Curaçao, terminating at a distant beach where you may go snorkeling and experience the underwater world.

Blue Finn Charters: This organization offers a combination of ATV rides and boat trips, allowing you to explore both land and sea. Their ATV ride takes you to the island's rugged north coast, while their boat tour delivers you to some of the top snorkeling sites surrounding Curaçao.

These are only a fraction of the different Jeep safari and ATV tour possibilities available in Curaçao. Whether you're an adrenaline junkie or just hunting for a fresh way to see the island, there's something for everyone.

Guided Hikes and Nature Walks

Whether you're interested in hiking, birdwatching, or simply enjoying the breathtaking natural beauty of the island, there are various tour firms available to help you organize your ideal adventure.

One popular tour organization is the **Curaçao Footprint Foundation**, which provides a choice of guided treks and nature excursions around the island's different landscapes. Their professional guides will take you to some of the most spectacular natural sites on the island, including national parks, beaches, and animal preserves. They offer various different trips to select from, including birding tours, history tours, and even night treks for a unique and amazing experience.

Another fantastic choice for guided hikes and nature excursions in Curaçao is the **Island Tour Centre.** They provide a choice of trips to select from, including guided walks through the Christoffel National Park and the Boka Tabla caves, as well as birding tours and snorkeling excursions. Their professional guides are enthusiastic about the island's natural beauty and fauna, and will take you to some of the most spectacular and remote areas on the island.

If you're searching for a more tailored hiking or nature trip experience, try contacting **Curaçao Actief,** a local tour agency that specializes in organizing customized excursions to fit your interests and requirements. Their skilled guides can construct a personalized itinerary depending on your tastes, whether you're interested in hiking, birding, or visiting the island's magnificent coastline.

There are lots of alternatives available for guided hikes and nature walks in Curaçao, so whether you're a nature fanatic or simply looking for a unique way to see the island, there's bound to be a tour agency that's suitable for you.

Boat Tours and Charters

Curaçao is a superb location for boat trips and charters, owing to its beautiful blue seas, varied marine life, and picturesque shoreline. Whether you're seeking to relax on a catamaran, discover secret beaches, or experience some of the greatest snorkeling and diving in the Caribbean, there are plenty of alternatives to pick from.

One popular choice is a **sailing excursion**, where you can appreciate the splendor of the coastline while feeling the wind in your hair.

Several firms offer sunset sailing cruises, where you may relax with a drink and watch the sun fall below the horizon. Some sailing trips also include pauses at snorkeling and bathing locations, so you may cool down in the pleasant seas.

If you're searching for a more personal experience, a **private boat charter** may be the way to go. You may select from a number of vessels, including catamarans, powerboats, and yachts, and construct your own bespoke route. Some charters offer guided snorkeling or diving trips, while others may concentrate more on relaxing and soaking up the sun.

For those who prefer to travel beyond the shoreline, there are also various boat cruises that transport you to surrounding islands or other sites of interest. One popular choice is a vacation to **Klein Curaçao**, a tiny deserted island famed for its stunning beaches and good snorkeling. Some excursions may include visits to sea turtle nesting places or bird observation locations.

Whatever style of boat trip or charter you pick, you're guaranteed to have a great time in the beautiful blue seas of Curaçao.

CHAPTER 6: GETTING AROUND IN CURAÇAO

Exploring the colorful culture, rich history, and magnificent beauty of Curaçao is a journey best enjoyed on wheels. With a plethora of transportation alternatives available, navigating this gorgeous island is an experience in itself.

Transportation Options

Curaçao offers several transportation alternatives available to guests, including taxis, rental autos, public buses, and private transports.

Taxis. Taxis are available on the island, and prices are regulated by the government. The fares are depending on the distance traveled and are calculated by a meter. Taxis are convenient and typically available, although they may be pricey, especially for longer outings. A typical cab from the airport to Willemstad, for example, may cost around **$30-$40.**

Rental cars: Rental cars are very generally available, and there are various international car rental corporations operating on the island. The rates for automotive rentals vary depending on the style of vehicle, rental length, and insurance coverage. A little car may cost around **$40-$50 per day,** whereas a larger SUV might cost around **$80-$100 per day.**

Buses: Public buses are the most cheap method for moving around in Curaçao, with fees ranging from **$1-$2 per route**. However, the bus routes are limited, and the buses may be full and uncomfortable, especially during peak hours.

Private transfers: Private transfers are another possibility for moving around in Curaçao, and they may be hired through hotels or travel organizations. The charges for private transfers vary depending on the distance traveled, however they could be more expensive than taxis or rental cars.

It's vital to note that driving in Curaça is on the right-hand side of the road, and the roads may be tiny and twisty. If you wish to rent a car, make sure you have a valid driver's license and are comfortable driving in unfamiliar settings. Additionally, be aware that parking could be hard, especially in Willemstad, where there is little space available.

Curaçao Offline Map

There are numerous choices for downloading an offline map of Curaçao on your mobile device. Here are a few suggestions:

Google Maps: The Google Maps app enables you to download maps of specified locations for offline usage. Just search for Curaçao, then click the download option.

Maps.me: This program includes comprehensive offline maps of cities and nations throughout the globe, including Curaçao. The app also includes places of interest and navigation functions.

Here WeGo: With this app, you can also download offline maps. Simply search for the area you wish to download, click the three dots in the upper right corner, then select "Download map" to download the map.

Having a map on hand may be a useful tool for touring Curaçao and discovering all that the island has to offer even without a data connection.

CHAPTER 7: WHERE TO STAY IN CURAÇAO

Choosing where to stay in Curaçao is like picking the hue of the Caribbean water; every choice is a stunning experience that will leave you spellbound.

Types of Lodging

Curaçao is a popular tourist destination with a wide range of lodging options to suit any budget or preference. Whether you're looking for a luxurious beachfront resort, a cozy bed and breakfast, or a simple hostel, Curaçao has something for everyone.

Hotels & Resorts:

Curaçao boasts a broad array of resorts that appeal to diverse interests and budgets. From magnificent five-star resorts to more economical alternatives, there is something for everyone.

Here are some popular resorts in Curaçao and their prices:

Santa Barbara Beach & Golf Resort:

Santa Barbara Beach & Golf Resort is a magnificent and serene hideaway situated on the southeast coast of Curaçao. It is set on 2,000 acres of magnificent beachfront land, surrounded by natural beauty and the crystal blue seas of the Caribbean Sea. The resort provides a choice of elegant accommodations, from big rooms to private villas, all intended to give the utmost in comfort and relaxation.

The resort's features include a championship golf course, a full-service spa, various dining choices, a private beach, and a range of water sports activities. The resort's primary restaurant, Shore, provides a magnificent beachside dining experience offering fresh seafood and international cuisine. The Medi Restaurant is recognized for its Mediterranean-inspired meals, while the Splash Pool Bar & Grill offers up casual food and tropical cocktails.

Santa Barbara Beach & Golf Resort provides different kinds of accommodations, including premium rooms, suites, and private villas. The deluxe accommodations have Caribbean-inspired décor and breathtaking views of the ocean or the resort's lush gardens. The suites are larger and have a separate sitting space and a balcony or patio with great views. The private villas provide the utmost in luxury and seclusion, offering a complete kitchen, a private pool, and various bedrooms and baths.

The resort has accessible accommodations, including wheelchair-accessible rooms, and public spaces are intended to be accessible as well. The resort amenities, such as the pool and spa, are accessible to visitors with disabilities. Staff members are also trained to help visitors with special needs, and are accessible 24/7 to ensure that all guests have a comfortable and pleasurable stay. In addition, the resort provides services such as transportation and excursions that are developed with accessibility in mind.

Prices for rooms at the Santa Barbara Beach & Golf Resort vary based on the season and the kind of accommodation picked. Deluxe accommodations start at roughly **$200** per night, while luxury villas may cost up to **$1,500** per night. The resort also provides all-inclusive packages that include meals, beverages, and select activities. You can get more information here;
https://www.santabarbararesortcuracao.com/

Avila Beach Hotel: Avila Beach Hotel is a luxury and historic resort situated in the Punda neighborhood of Willemstad, Curaçao. Originally established in 1780, the hotel has been significantly refurbished and enlarged to give contemporary facilities while keeping its colonial elegance.

The hotel provides a choice of accommodation types, including regular rooms, suites, and villas, all of which are attractively designed and equipped with contemporary facilities such as air conditioning, free Wi-Fi, and flat-screen TVs. Some rooms additionally include balconies or patios with ocean views.

The Avila Beach Hotel boasts two private beaches, three swimming pools, a fitness center, a full-service spa, and several on-site dining options, including the Belle Terrace restaurant, which serves contemporary international cuisine, and the Blues Bar & Restaurant, which offers live music and Caribbean-inspired dishes.

In terms of accessibility, the Avila Beach Hotel is totally wheelchair accessible, featuring ramps and elevators throughout the resort. The hotel also features certain rooms that are expressly constructed to assist visitors with disabilities, featuring roll-in showers and grab bars.

The Avila Beach Hotel is a popular option for both leisure and business tourists, with its ideal location, outstanding facilities, and impeccable service. Prices for accommodations vary based on the season and room type, but start at roughly

$200 per night. You will get more information here; https://www.avilabeachhotel.com/

Sunscape Curaçao Resort, Spa & Casino

Sunscape Curaçao Resort, Spa & Casino is a beachfront all-inclusive resort nestled in the gorgeous Piscadera Bay. This resort provides comfortable rooms, tasty eating choices, engaging activities, and entertainment for all ages.

The resort features a total of 341 guest rooms and suites, each boasting an own balcony or patio with spectacular ocean, garden or pool views. The rooms are furnished with contemporary facilities like flat-screen TVs, mini-fridges, and coffee machines.

Sunscape Curaçao Resort features six restaurants, including buffet and à la carte selections, featuring foreign cuisine such as Italian, Mexican, and Caribbean. There are also five bars, including a swim-up bar and a beach bar, serving a range of drinks and beverages.

The resort provides many activities for visitors to enjoy, including kayaking, paddleboarding, snorkeling, and scuba diving. There is also a fitness center, tennis courts, and a spa providing a variety of services.

For families, the resort includes a kids' club and a teen club with age-appropriate activities and entertainment. There is also a casino on-site for those seeking for some excitement.

The costs for a stay at Sunscape Curaçao Resort, Spa & Casino might vary based on the season and the kind of accommodation picked. However, rates normally vary from roughly **$200** to **$500** each night. The all-inclusive package includes meals, beverages, and activities.

In terms of accessibility for visitors with impairments, The resort provides wheelchair-accessible rooms with expanded entrances, lowered light switches and temperature controls, and roll-in showers with grab bars. The resort's public facilities, including restaurants, bars, and swimming pools, are also handicapped accessible. Additionally, the resort includes accessible parking spots and ramps around the site. You will get more information here; https://www.sunscaperesorts.com/Curaçao

Renaissance Curaçao Resort & Casino:

The Renaissance Curaçao Resort & Casino is a magnificent hotel situated in the center of Willemstad, the capital city of Curaçao. The hotel features 237 contemporary and large rooms and suites, each of which is equipped with all the essential conveniences to provide a pleasant stay.

The rooms are furnished in a modern manner and have a private balcony or patio, a flat-screen TV, air conditioning, a mini-fridge, and a private bathroom with a shower or bathtub. Guests may pick between ocean or city views based on their desire.

The resort has a broad choice of eating options accessible, including the on-site restaurant, Nautilus, which provides both local and foreign cuisine. Additionally, there are various pubs and lounges on the resort where visitors may relax and have a drink.

For guests wishing to rest and unwind, the resort has a huge outdoor swimming pool surrounded by a wide sun deck and loungers. The on-site fitness facility and full-service spa give options to be active and rejuvenate.

The Renaissance Curaçao Resort & Casino is also renowned for its casino, where visitors may try their luck at numerous games like slot machines, poker, and blackjack.

The hotel is strategically positioned near several of Willemstad's prominent attractions, including the Queen Emma Bridge, the Mikve Israel-Emanuel Synagogue, and the Curaçao Maritime Museum. Additionally, the resort provides free shuttle service to and from the neighboring Mambo Beach Boulevard, where visitors may enjoy shopping, eating, and entertainment opportunities.

Regarding accessibility, the Renaissance Curaçao Resort & Casino has wheelchair accessible rooms and public places, with elevators provided for easy access to various levels. The hotel staff is also trained to help visitors with impairments to guarantee a pleasant and pleasurable stay for all customers. Prices vary from **$200-$400** per night. You will get more information from here;

Hilton Curaçao:

Hilton Curaçao is a spectacular oceanfront resort located on the Piscadera Bay in Willemstad, the capital city of Curaçao. The resort has a wonderful view of the Caribbean Sea and is surrounded by lush tropical gardens. The hotel's position is ideal for travelers who seek to enjoy the island's attractions.

The rooms and suites of the Hilton Curaçao are modern and big, with tropical-inspired décor and a range of services to assure a pleasurable stay. All rooms offer private balconies or patios with a view of the gardens or the sea, and guests may choose from a range of accommodation choices to suit their preferences and interests.

The resort features two private beaches, excellent for swimming, sunbathing, or trying out water sports such as snorkeling, kayaking, and scuba diving. The resort's infinity pool is also a popular spot for guests to relax and enjoy the spectacular views of the ocean.

Hilton Curaçao has a number of eating selections to suit all tastes and occasions. Guests may taste Caribbean and international cuisine at the Aqua Restaurant, eat fresh seafood at the Cielo Restaurant, or relax with a drink at the bar by the pool. There is also a coffee shop and a convenience store for anyone who needs a quick snack or refreshment.

The resort features a variety of facilities to cater to tourists' wants and interests. There is a highly equipped exercise center, a spa giving massages and beauty treatments, and a casino for those who prefer to try their luck. The resort also has a Kids Club, offering activities and entertainment for children, making it a fantastic alternative for families.

Hilton Curaçao is devoted to making its facilities accessible to all visitors, especially those with impairments. The resort provides accessible rooms and public locations, and personnel are trained to give support to tourists with disabilities. The resort's website includes information on its accessible features, and guests are invited to contact the hotel directly to discuss their needs and preferences.

The rates at Hilton Curaçao vary depending on the time of year and the hotel type selected. However, guests may anticipate to pay around **$200-$400** per night for a standard lodging. You will get more information here;

Papagayo Beach Resort:

Papagayo Beach Resort is a magnificent beachfront resort located on Jan Thiel Bay, one of the most popular sites in Curaçao. The resort includes a selection of spacious and modern rooms, suites, and villas, all with either a garden, pool, or ocean view. The rooms are created with a contemporary style, and they are equipped with modern comforts such as air conditioning, free Wi-Fi, flat-screen TVs, and a minibar.

The resort offers a spacious outdoor pool surrounded by sun loungers, and a quiet beach area with crystal-clear oceans and lovely sand. Guests may also enjoy a variety of water activities such as snorkeling, diving, and kayaking. The resort has an on-site restaurant that serves a selection of international and local dishes, as well as a beach bar where guests may enjoy refreshing drinks.

For those who like to keep active, the resort has a fitness center, tennis facilities, and an adjacent golf course. The resort also features a spa and wellness center where guests may enjoy a range of treatments and massages. There is a kids' club on-site, which gives children a selection of activities to keep them occupied during their stay.

Papagayo Beach Resort is a popular choice for guests seeking a tranquil beach vacation in Curaçao. The resort's facilities, location, and personal service make it a wonderful destination for families, couples, and lone guests. The resort is also focused on accessibility and offers rooms and services for people with disabilities. Prices range from **$150-$400** per night. You will get more information here;
https://www.papagayobeachresort.com/

Curaçao Marriott Beach Resort:

Curaçao Marriott Beach Resort is a magnificent resort situated on the Piscadera Bay in

Willemstad, Curaçao. The resort features amazing views of the ocean, a private beach, and lush tropical flora. It affords tourists an escape to paradise with its great service, rich amenities, and pleasant accommodations.

The resort features a range of rooms and suites, all of which are elegantly equipped with modern furniture, sumptuous bedding, and Caribbean-inspired décor. Each room comes with its individual balcony or patio, giving stunning views of the ocean or the resort's tropical plants.

Guests may enjoy a number of on-site amenities, including three outdoor swimming pools, a fitness center, and a full-service spa. The resort also offers a variety of eating alternatives, from simple poolside dining to elegant dining at the property's eponymous restaurant, Portofino.

For those who prefer to explore the island, the resort is positioned adjacent to several attractions, including the historic city center of

Willemstad, the Curaçao Sea Aquarium, and the Hato Caves. The resort also features a range of activities, including snorkeling, diving, and hiking.

The Curaçao Marriott Beach Resort is also a fantastic place for weddings and events, with its breathtaking ocean views, beautiful tropical gardens, and modern event facilities. The resort's event planning department is ready to help guests plan and execute their dream occasion.

Prices for stays at the Curaçao Marriott Beach Resort varies depending on the season and room type. However, guests may anticipate to pay around **$300** per night for a standard lodging.

Curaçao Marriott Beach Resort has accessible facilities for tourists with disabilities. The resort features accessible guest rooms with amenities such as roll-in showers, grab bars, and lowered bathroom fittings. In addition, the resort has accessible public places, including the lobby, restaurants, and fitness center. The site also includes wheelchair-accessible means of travel to and from parking spots, as well as accessible beach parts. Guests with unique accessibility requirements are advised to contact the resort in advance of their stay to ensure that their needs may be met.

These fees are subject to fluctuation depending on the time of year and availability, so it is best to check with each resort for the most up-to-date pricing information here; https://www.marriott.com/hotels/travel/curbr-renaissance-curacao-resort-and-casino/

Villas And Vacation Rentals:

Curaçao is home to numerous gorgeous villas and vacation rentals, making it a fantastic choice for those wishing a more private and sophisticated escape. Here are a few available villas and holiday rentals in Curaçao, along with their prices:

Villa Royale: Villa Royale is a wonderful vacation property in Curaçao that provides travelers a superb combination of luxury, seclusion, and serenity. This spectacular villa is situated in the premium residential enclave of Vista Royal in Jan Thiel, which is famous for its lovely beaches, vibrant environment, and closeness to prominent restaurants, clubs, and enterprises.

The villa features six big bedrooms, each with its own en-suite bathroom, making it a perfect option for large families, groups of friends, or business vacations. The bedrooms are air-conditioned and enjoy excellent views of the surrounding landscape. The villa's interiors are attractively designed with contemporary furniture and local art pieces, giving a warm and friendly ambiance.

The home also boasts a fully equipped gourmet kitchen, a wonderful living room, and a separate dining space that can seat up to 12 people. The outdoor living areas are likewise spectacular, with a huge pool, a covered patio, and a wide sun deck with lounge chairs and umbrellas. The property also includes a BBQ patio, making it excellent for hosting guests.

The villa crew comprises a daily maid, gardener, and pool maintenance pros, ensuring that visitors have a stress-free and comfortable stay. The villa's concierge service may also help plan airport transfers, vehicle rentals, restaurant reservations, and other activities to ensure visitors have a good stay.

The rental pricing for Villa Royale begins at **$1,200** per night, and it can accommodate up to 12 people. The cost includes daily cleaning, Wi-Fi, cable TV, and other amenities. Additional luxuries like chef services, spa treatments, and tour guides may be booked for an additional charge. Prices start at roughly **$500** per night. You will get more information here; https://www.villaroyalecuracao.com/

Coral Estate Villas: Coral Estate Villas is a lovely and unique resort located on the west coast of Curaçao, featuring individual villas and apartments with fantastic ocean views. The homes are located on a hillside overlooking the Caribbean Sea and surrounded by gorgeous tropical gardens.

The villas in Coral Estate are created with the utmost comfort and leisure in mind. They offer big living areas, modern kitchens, and vast outdoor patios with private pools or hot tubs. Each villa is elegantly built and supplied with high-end conveniences, such air conditioning, flat-screen TVs, and complimentary Wi-Fi.

The resort offers a number of accommodation solutions to fit varied party sizes and tastes, from one-bedroom apartments to six-bedroom villas. The villas are perfect for families, couples, and groups of friends seeking for a stunning and quiet retreat in Curaçao.

In addition to the stunning houses, Coral Estate also has a breathtaking infinity pool overlooking the ocean, a private beach club, and an excellent restaurant providing great meals made with fresh local ingredients. The resort also features a variety of activities, including snorkeling, kayaking, and paddleboarding.

Coral Estate Villas in Curaçao is a luxury vacation rental resort located on the island's western coast. With amazing ocean views, a private beach, and beautiful gardens, it's the perfect environment for a quiet weekend.

In terms of accessibility, Coral Estate Villas has various wheelchair-friendly accommodations, including one-bedroom villas with roll-in showers and grab bars in the bathroom. The facility also offers a beach wheelchair with big wheels that can easily manage sand and difficult terrain, allowing those with mobility issues to enjoy the beach.

In addition to wheelchair-friendly accommodations, Coral Estate Villas also features a restaurant and bar on site, both of which are accessible. The restaurant provides both indoor and outdoor eating places, and the bar has plenty of capacity for wheelchairs.

Rates for the villas at Coral Estate vary depending on the season and the size of the villa, with rates starting at around **$200** per night for a one-bedroom apartment and ranging up to **$1,500** per night for a six-bedroom villa during peak season. The resort also offers special packages and discounts throughout the year. You will get more information here;
https://www.coralestatevillas.com/

Blue Bay Villa: Blue Bay Villa is a stunning and huge vacation villa located in the exclusive Blue Bay Golf and Beach Resort in Curaçao. The property is perfect for families or groups of friends who desire to spend a luxurious and enjoyable stay in the Caribbean.

The property offers four bedrooms, all with en-suite bathrooms, air conditioning, and ceiling fans. The master bedroom also has a Jacuzzi tub and a walk-in closet. The home can accommodate up to eight guests and features a big living room, dining area, and fully equipped kitchen.

Outside, there is a private pool and terrace with sun loungers, a grill area, and an outdoor dining space. The home also boasts wonderful views of the golf course and the Caribbean Sea.

The Blue Bay Golf and Beach Resort is a gated community that offers a variety of services, including a private beach, golf course, tennis courts, and a fitness center. The resort is located within a 10-minute drive from Willemstad, the capital of Curaçao, and is accessible to numerous other beaches, restaurants, and activities.

The price for renting the Blue Bay Villa varies depending on the time of year and the length of stay. However, on average, the rental charge is roughly **$500** per night.

Boca Gentil Villas: Boca Gentil Villas is a magnificent oceanfront villa complex located in Jan Thiel, one of the most sought-after neighborhoods of Curaçao. The complex has a range of villas with spectacular views of the Caribbean Sea, huge living areas, and luxury conveniences for a superb vacation experience.

Each villa is creatively designed and decorated with a contemporary Caribbean flair, and comes equipped with modern appliances, air conditioning, and high-speed Wi-Fi. The villas include a choice of arrangements, ranging from one to five bedrooms, making it excellent for couples, families, and huge parties. Guests may choose from a variety of villa options, including Garden Villas, Sea View Villas, and Oceanfront Villas.

Boca Gentil Villas offers a multitude of amenities to guarantee tourists a memorable and comfortable stay, including a private beach club with lounge chairs, a restaurant, and bar, as well as access to a fitness center, spa, and concierge services. Guests may also take advantage of the adjoining Jan Thiel Beach, where they may swim, sunbathe, and enjoy a range of water sports.

The pricing of the villas at Boca Gentil Villas vary depending on the size and kind of the villa, as well as the season of year. Prices generally range from **$500 to $2000** per night, and tourists may take advantage of special packages and discounts to acquire the greatest value for their stay.

Boca Gentil Villas are accessible for persons with limitations. The villas offer wide doors, accessible bathrooms with grab bars, and other facilities that make them easier to maintain. Some of the villas additionally have wheelchair ramps and elevators for visitors who need them.

In addition to the accessible hotels, the area includes a range of services that appeal to guests with disabilities. The neighborhood provides an on-site restaurant and bar, as well as a spa and workout facilities. The staff is also trained to offer help to customers with disabilities, including arranging for accessible transportation and excursions. You will get more information from here; https://www.bocagentilvillas.com/

Kas Kinikini: Kas Kinikini is a stunning beachfront vacation rental home located in the affluent region of Jan Thiel in Curaçao. With four bedrooms and four bathrooms, it can accommodate up to eight guests comfortably. The house is created with a modern and tropical style, presenting tourists with a pleasant and serene location.

The property has a big living and dining room that extends out to a covered terrace overlooking the Caribbean Sea. The terrace is perfect for al fresco dining, resting, and viewing the spectacular sunsets. The house also offers a fully equipped kitchen with modern conveniences, including a dishwasher and a Nespresso machine.

The bedrooms at Kas Kinikini are all air-conditioned and come with ensuite bathrooms. The main bedroom has a king-size bed, a walk-in closet, and a private balcony overlooking the sea. The remaining bedrooms include either a queen-size or two twin-size beds, making the villa excellent for families or groups of friends.

Outside, the residence offers a beautiful infinity pool with a wide sun patio and comfortable lounge furniture. There is also a private staircase leading down to the beach, where guests may enjoy swimming, snorkeling, and other water activities.

Kas Kinikini is available for hire year-round, although rates vary according to the season. Prices start at around **$700** per night, and discounts are available for prolonged stays. The house is professionally kept and comes with daily cleaning, a private chef upon request, and 24/7 concierge service to help customers schedule their activities and experiences in Curaçao.

No matter the villa or vacation rental you chose, you're certain to enjoy a magnificent and amazing experience in Curaçao.

Bed and Breakfasts

These hotels are typically family-owned and create a cozy atmosphere with extra attention from the hosts. Here are numerous Bed and Breakfasts that come highly recommended and their prices:

Bed and Breakfast Blenchi - Bed and Breakfast Blenchi is a modest and rustic hideaway nestled in the countryside of Curaçao, just a short drive from the island's stunning beaches and attractions. This wonderful bed & breakfast is housed in a historic plantation property that goes back to the 18th century, and has been lovingly rebuilt to create comfortable and authentic rooms for tourists.

The resort contains three guest rooms, each of which is distinctively furnished with traditional island furniture and vibrant decorations. The rooms are big and open, with high ceilings, enormous windows, and abundance of natural light. Amenities include air conditioning, free Wi-Fi, and private bathrooms.

Outside, guests may relax on the spacious veranda and enjoy the views of the nearby gardens and environment. The residence also has a swimming pool and sun deck, as well as a barbecue area and outdoor dining space.

Breakfast is included in the lodging fee, and is given daily on the terrace or in the dining room. Guests may enjoy a choice of fresh fruits, breads, pastries, and local specialties, as well as coffee, tea, and juice.

Bed & Breakfast Blenchi offers a calm and unique refuge for those who seek to experience the natural beauty and charm of Curaçao. Prices start at **$90** per night.

<u>Bed and Breakfast La Creole</u> - Bed and Breakfast La Creole is a nice and comfortable destination to stay while traveling the island of Curaçao. Located in the historic district of Pietermaai in Willemstad, this 19th-century property has been lovingly refurbished and transformed into a modest bed & breakfast with six guest rooms.

Each room at La Creole is creatively designed with Caribbean-style furnishings and has a private bathroom, air conditioning, and free Wi-Fi. Some rooms further offer a balcony or patio with views of the city or the sea.

Guests may have a fantastic breakfast each morning on the outdoor terrace, which overlooks the pool and tropical flora. The B&B also offers a small bar where guests may enjoy a drink or a snack.

La Creole is just a short walk from many of Willemstad's greatest sights, including the old forts and colorful buildings of Punda and Otrobanda. The bed and breakfast also offers free parking for tourists who desire to rent a car and explore the island on their own.

Bed & Breakfast La Creole is a great solution for anyone seeking a nice and handy area to stay in Curaçao. Prices for a room start at around **$100** per night.

Scuba Lodge & Ocean Suites - Scuba Lodge & Ocean Suites is a magnificent boutique hotel located in the famous Pietermaai area of Willemstad, the capital of Curaçao. The hotel is positioned on the coast and has magnificent views of the Caribbean Sea. Scuba Lodge & Ocean Suites is housed in a historic building that has been elegantly refurbished and features a blend of traditional Caribbean architecture and modern design.

The hotel includes 28 rooms and suites, each furnished with unique Caribbean flair and fitted with modern comforts such as air conditioning, Wi-Fi, and flat-screen TVs. The rooms are spacious and comfortable, with plenty of natural light and trendy décor.

Scuba Lodge & Ocean Suites is notably popular with scuba divers and snorkelers, as the hotel has its own dive center that offers a range of courses and guided dives. Guests may also enjoy a range of other water sports, including kayaking, stand-up paddleboarding, and fishing. The hotel's oceanfront pool is a lovely spot to relax and soak up the sun, and there are plenty of loungers and umbrellas for guests to enjoy.

The hotel's restaurant, which is open for breakfast, lunch, and supper, provides a mix of Caribbean and international cuisine. The restaurant also has a bar, where customers may enjoy a selection of cocktails, beers, and wines.

Scuba Lodge & Ocean Suites is a terrific solution for travelers seeking a comfortable and convenient hotel in Curaçao. The hotel's location in the Pietermaai district puts it adjacent to some of the top restaurants, bars, and shopping in Willemstad, and the hotel's cheerful and helpful staff are always on hand to assist guests organize their stay. Prices start at **$125** per night.

The Ritz Village Hotel - The Ritz Village Hotel is a wonderful hotel located in the downtown of Willemstad, Curaçao's capital city. This hotel was first intended as a school in the 19th century and has been stylishly restored while retaining its historic splendor. The hotel has excellent accommodations with a number of room types to choose from, including private rooms, studios, and apartments.

All rooms are air-conditioned and equipped with a private bathroom, free Wi-Fi, a flat-screen TV, and a kitchenette with a fridge and coffee maker. The hotel also offers a spectacular outdoor pool, a fitness center, a restaurant, and a bar.

The Ritz Village Hotel is located within walking distance of some of the city's important attractions, including the colorful Handelskade, the historic Fort Amsterdam, and the floating market. The hotel also offers free shuttle service to the beach, making it a perfect choice for beach aficionados.

The hotel is also recognized for its exceptional service, with cheerful people who are always willing to assist with any requests or concerns tourists may have. Whether you're here for business or vacation, The Ritz Village Hotel delivers a unique and delightful stay in the middle of Curaçao. Prices start at **$65** per night.

<u>Adonai Hotel Boutique</u> - Adonai Hotel Boutique is a trendy and pleasant lodging choice situated in the center of Willemstad, Curaçao. This modest boutique hotel features just nine rooms, each distinctively designed with local art and furniture, providing a warm and welcome ambiance for visitors.

The hotel provides a selection of facilities, including a rooftop terrace with a Jacuzzi and lounge chairs, great for soaking up the sun and enjoying panoramic views of the city. Guests may also relax in the hotel's outdoor pool or enjoy a massage or other spa treatments.

Rooms at Adonai Hotel Boutique are air-conditioned and include private balconies, flat-screen TVs, and complementary Wi-Fi. The hotel also serves a free breakfast each morning, comprising fresh local fruits, bread, and pastries.

The hotel is situated within a short walk from the historic core of Willemstad, a UNESCO World Heritage Site. Guests may easily explore the city's vivid streets and colorful architecture, as well as visit neighboring sites like the Hato Caves or the Curaçao Sea Aquarium.

Adonai Hotel Boutique is a fantastic alternative for guests searching for a unique and pleasant place to stay in Curaçao, with individual care and attention to detail. Prices start at **$110** per night.

These Bed & Breakfasts provide a variety of services like breakfast, free Wi-Fi, and swimming pools. Their customized attention and warm environment are guaranteed to make your visit in Curaçao a memorable one.

Hostels:

Curaçao provides a selection of hostels that are great for budget-conscious guests who yet want to enjoy the island's rich culture and attractions. Here are some ideas for hostels and their costs in Curaçao:

Hostel La Creole - Hostel La Creole is a lovely hostel situated in the center of Willemstad, the capital city of Curaçao. It is located in a wonderfully renovated building that dates back to the 1800s and is only a few steps away from the busy Pietermaai District. The hostel includes comfortable dormitory-type rooms and private rooms, all of which are designed in a vibrant and colorful Caribbean manner.

The dormitory-style rooms at Hostel La Creole are great for budget-conscious tourists who are searching for an economical but pleasant place to stay. These rooms can accommodate up to six people and come with private lockers for each visitor. The private rooms, on the other hand, are great for couples or small groups that want a bit more solitude. These rooms are furnished with air conditioning, a private toilet, and a small kitchenette.

Hostel La Creole also features numerous community places where guests may rest and interact. The hostel boasts a wide courtyard with lots of lounging places and a BBQ grill, as well as a rooftop terrace that gives great views of the city. There is also a shared kitchen where visitors may cook their own meals, as well as a nice sitting space with a TV and a small library.

The costs of Hostel La Creole are quite reasonable and vary based on the kind of accommodation and the season. Dormitory-style accommodations start at roughly **$20** per night per person, while private rooms start at around **$60** per night for two people. These rates include free Wi-Fi and a continental breakfast. Hostel La Creole also provides discounts for longer stays, making it a good alternative for tourists who are searching for an extended stay in Curaçao.

City Hostel Curaçao - City Hostel Curaçao is a comfortable and economical lodging choice situated in the center of Willemstad, the capital city of Curaçao. The hostel provides both private rooms and dormitory-style accommodations, making it a fantastic alternative for lone travelers, couples, and groups. The rooms are clean, large, and equipped with comfy mattresses, air conditioning, and free Wi-Fi.

City Hostel Curaçao features a casual and welcoming environment, and visitors may enjoy mingling in the common facilities, which include a communal kitchen, living room, and outdoor patio. The hostel also serves complimentary breakfast, coffee, and tea to all guests.

The location of the hostel is one of its greatest qualities, since it is located in the busy Pietermaai neighborhood, renowned for its colorful colonial buildings, fashionable restaurants, and dynamic nightlife. The hostel is also only a short walk away from the city's historic downtown area and the famed Pontoon Bridge.

Prices for dormitory-style lodging at City Hostel Curaçao start at roughly **$20** per night, making it an excellent budget-friendly alternative for tourists visiting the island. Private rooms are also available at higher pricing, but still provide excellent value for money compared to other hotel alternatives on the island.

<u>Poppy Hostel</u> - Poppy Hostel is a budget-friendly lodging choice situated in the middle of Willemstad, the capital city of Curaçao. It provides both dormitory-style and private rooms, making it an excellent alternative for lone travelers, backpackers, and groups of friends. The hostel is set in a beautiful colonial-style structure that dates back to the 18th century and is only a few minutes' walk from the city's major attractions, including the floating market, the Queen Emma Bridge, and the historic neighborhood of Punda.

Poppy Hostel features a cheerful and inviting environment, with a common room where guests may rest and chat with one other. There is also a fully equipped kitchen where visitors may cook their own meals, as well as a small on-site bar that sells beverages and snacks. The hostel provides free Wi-Fi throughout the property, and there is also a small outside courtyard where guests may enjoy the Caribbean weather.

The costs at Poppy Hostel are quite reasonable, making it an excellent alternative for budget-conscious tourists. Dormitory-style accommodations start at roughly **$20** per night, while private rooms start at around **$50** per night. The hostel also provides discounts for long-term stays, making it a wonderful alternative for tourists who are wanting to spend an extended amount of time in Curaçao.

<u>Bed & Bike Curaçao</u> - Bed & Bike Curaçao is a quiet and lovely hostel situated in the center of Willemstad, the capital city of Curaçao. The hostel is great for tourists who are searching for a cheap and eco-friendly housing alternative. As the name indicates, the hotel provides bicycles for hire, making it easier for visitors to explore the island at their own leisure.

Bed & Bike Curaçao provides a range of lodging choices, including dorm dorms and private rooms. The dorm rooms may sleep up to six people and are fitted with bunk beds, personal lockers, and fans. The private rooms come with either a double bed or two single beds, and include a private bathroom, air conditioning, and a balcony.

The hostel features a shared kitchen where visitors may cook their own meals, as well as a nice lounge room where guests can rest and mingle. There is also a rooftop patio where visitors may enjoy the wonderful views of the city.

The costs at Bed & Bike Curaçao are quite fair and competitive, making it a perfect alternative for budget tourists. The hostel also provides several packages, including a bike rental package and a diving package; rates start at roughly **$30** per night for a dormitory bed, and private rooms are also available.

Happy Turtle Hostel - Happy Turtle Hostel is a cute and friendly hostel located in the center of the Pietermaai District, one of the most vibrant areas of Willemstad. The hostel offers a bright and pleasant ambiance that symbolizes the laid-back tropical sentiments of Curaçao.

The Happy Turtle Hostel has lovely shared dormitory rooms and private rooms, all equipped with air conditioning and free Wi-Fi. The hostel features a communal kitchen, where guests may cook their meals, as well as a wonderful common room with soft chairs and hammocks to relax and meet other travelers.

The hostel's location is perfect for guests who desire to explore the city on foot, because it is adjacent to various bars, restaurants, and landmarks, including the historic Queen Emma Bridge and the Floating Market. The crew is polite and always glad to help travelers with any concerns they may have about the island.

The rates at Happy Turtle Hostel are inexpensive and deliver outstanding value for money. The hostel is a fantastic solution for budget-conscious travelers who seek to learn the local culture and engage with like-minded folks.

Prices start at around **$20** per night for a dormitory bed, and private rooms are also available.

Whatever your preference or budget, Curaçao gives a number of accommodation possibilities to pick from, ensuring you enjoy a comfortable and happy stay on the island.

Best Areas to Stay

Here are some of the top sites to stay in Curaçao:

Willemstad: The capital city of Curaçao is a notable site for travelers. Willemstad is famous for its beautiful Dutch colonial architecture, superb restaurants, and bustling nightlife. There are lots of different accomodation alternatives in Willemstad, ranging from luxury hotels to budget-friendly guesthouses.

Pietermaai: Pietermaai is a trendy neighborhood located just east of Willemstad. It is home to various fine restaurants, bars, and clubs, making it a fantastic spot for nightlife fans. There are also dozens of boutique hotels and holiday flats in Pietermaai.

Jan Thiel: Jan Thiel is a coastal community located southeast of Willemstad. It is home to a gorgeous beach, several exceptional restaurants, and a variety of water sports and activities. Jan Thiel is a lovely area for families and couples seeking a more calm atmosphere.

Westpunt: If you're searching for a more quiet and tranquil setting, Westpunt might be the ideal solution. It is located on the northwestern part of the island and is famous for its magnificent beaches, crystal-clear oceans, and superb diving opportunities.

Scharloo: Scharloo is another old area in Willemstad that is famous for its spectacular architecture. It is a quieter zone than some of the other regions in Willemstad, making it a perfect choice for persons who prefer to stay near the core of the city but still enjoy a tranquil setting.

No matter the area you choose to stay in, Curaçao is certain to impress with its stunning beaches, rich culture, and warm hospitality.

Budgeting and Booking Tips

Curaçao is an amazing holiday place for people with varying budgets. Here are some budgeting and booking ideas to bear in mind while searching for accommodation:

Determine your budget: Before reserving any hotel, it is necessary to identify how much you are ready to spend on lodging. This can help you limit down your alternatives and prevent overpaying.

Book in early: Booking your hotel well in advance may help you save money. Many hotels and vacation rentals offer early bird rates, so take advantage of this and book your stay as soon as you can.

Look for offers and discounts: Check hotel and vacation rental websites for promotional deals, coupon codes, or discounts. You may also explore reserving via online travel companies like Expedia, reserving.com, or Airbnb, which frequently offer cheaper pricing than booking directly with the hotel.

Consider the location: Staying in the midst of the activity could be attractive, but it is frequently more costly. Consider lodging in less touristic places, which may be more economical.

check rates: It's crucial to check costs between various motels to locate the greatest bargain. Don't forget to weigh in the facilities and location while making your pick.

Check for alternative accommodation: If you're on a limited budget, investigate alternatives to standard hotels, such as hostels, bed & breakfasts, or vacation rentals.

Travel during off-peak season: Accommodation costs frequently reduce during the off-peak season when there are less visitors. If you're flexible with your trip dates, try going during this period to save money on hotels.

By keeping these guidelines in mind, you can locate economical hotels in Curaçao and have more money to spend on experiences and activities throughout your vacation.

Accommodation Agencies in Curaçao

Some of the most popular housing agencies in Curaçao include:

Booking.com: This is one of the most prominent online booking sites that provides a broad choice of lodging alternatives in Curaçao. You may visit their official website at https://www.booking.com/

Airbnb: This web platform provides a range of unique lodgings, including flats, villas, and private rooms.you may visit their official website at www.airbnb.com

Expedia: This is another popular online booking site that provides a broad choice of lodging alternatives in Curaçao. You may visit their official website at www.expedia.com

Curaçao Hospitality & tourist group (CHATA): This is a non-profit group that represents the tourist industry in Curaçao and provides a list of hotels on its website. you may visit their official website at https://www.chata.org/

Island Time Curaçao: This is a local travel service that provides bespoke vacation packages and can help you choose lodgings depending on your requirements and tastes.

When planning your lodgings in Curaçao, it's crucial to consider things such as location, facilities, and pricing. Be sure to book in early to obtain the greatest discounts and availability. Additionally, it's a good idea to read reviews and check out images of lodgings before reserving to verify that they suit your expectations.

CHAPTER 8: FOOD AND DRINK IN CURAÇAO

Discover the colorful and vibrant flavors of Curaçao, where the fusion of European, African, and Caribbean influences come together in a mouth-watering symphony of taste and tradition.

Local Cuisine and Specialties

Curaçao's indigenous cuisine is a unique blend of African, European, and Caribbean flavors that are certain to thrill your taste buds. Here are some of the must-try dishes in Curaçao:

Krioyo Cuisine

Krioyo cuisine is the traditional meal of Curaçao that has been influenced by different cultures such as Dutch, Spanish, African, and Portuguese. Krioyo, which means 'local' in Papiamentu, the indigenous language of Curaçao, is a cuisine that marries the best of Caribbean and Latin American ingredients with a unique twist.

One of the most popular dishes in Krioyo cuisine is **'Keshi Yena'**, which is a cheese ball stuffed with spiced meat, vegetables, and sometimes prunes or raisins. Other popular dishes include **'Sopi Mondongo'**, a tripe soup filled with vegetables, herbs, and spices, and **'Stoba'**, a hearty stew made with beef, chicken, or goat.

Seafood is also an important component of Krioyo cuisine, with dishes like **'Funchi ku hasa'**, a fish dish that is served with polenta and pan-fried plantains. **'Kabritu Stoba',** a goat stew, is another traditional food that is often served with rice and beans.

In addition to the main meals, Krioyo cuisine also comprises a variety of side dishes, including **'Funchi'**, a polenta-like dish prepared with cornmeal, and **'Yuana'**, a dish created with iguana meat that is cooked with onions, tomatoes, and spices.

For dessert, Krioyo cuisine features a range of sweet pleasures, such as **'Bolo di Manteka'**, a butter cake that is flavored with cinnamon and nutmeg, and **'Bolo Pretu',** a dark, spiced cake that is frequently served at weddings and other major occasions.

Dutch Influences

As a former Dutch colony, Curaçao has a unique blend of European and Caribbean influences, particularly in its cuisine. The Dutch influence may be visible in numerous local meals that are presented in restaurants across the island.

One renowned Dutch-influenced food is **'Stamppot'**, a big mashed potato dish that is often served with a vegetable like kale or sauerkraut and a form of smoked sausage. Another renowned dinner is **'Bitterballen'**, a tasty fried snack filled with a combination of beef or veal ragout and garnished with mustard.

The Dutch also brought with them their legendary **'poffertjes**,' small fluffy pancakes that are served with butter and powdered sugar. Another beloved Dutch pleasure is **'stroopwafels**,' miniature waffles constructed from two layers of fried dough and filled with caramel syrup.

Visitors visiting Curaçao may experience these and other Dutch-influenced food at several restaurants and cafés across the island.

Seafood and Fish Dishes

Some of the popular seafood and fish dishes in Curaçao include:

Grilled lobster - Curaçao is known for its succulent and delectable lobster, which is often grilled and served with a side of rice and beans or a fresh salad.

Fish soup - Made with a blend of fresh fish, veggies, and spices, this hearty and tasty soup is a beloved lunch in Curaçao. It is typically served with a side of bread or crackers.

Stewed fish - Another favorite fish dinner in Curaçao is stewed fish, which is produced using a mix of fresh fish, vegetables, and herbs cooked in a rich tomato-based sauce.

Conch salad - This wonderful and light salad contains thinly sliced conch meat combined with onions, peppers, and tomatoes, all tossed in a citrus dressing.

Fish cakes - These tasty and crispy cakes are prepared using a mix of fish, potatoes, onions, and spices, formed into small patties and fried until golden brown.

Shrimp sate - This dinner features juicy grilled shrimp skewered with peppers and onions, and served with a peanut dipping sauce.

Curaçao's seafood is best enjoyed at one of the many local restaurants and beachside cafés that dot the island, where you can soak in the magnificent panoramas while savoring the island's superb cuisine.

Fine Dining

Curaçao is a destination for food connoisseurs with many amazing restaurants and dining selections to choose from. If you're seeking for a terrific eating experience, there are several eateries that you should surely check out.

One of the main selections is **NAO Restaurant**, located in the fashionable Pietermaai district. The restaurant serves a blend of Caribbean and Asian food, with a focus on employing fresh, local products. The menu features items such as seared tuna, miso-marinated pork belly, and wagyu beef.

Another wonderful choice is **Baoase Culinary Beach Restaurant**, nestled on a stunning private beach. The restaurant delivers French and Asian-inspired meals and has an extensive wine collection. Signature dinners include the truffle risotto and the Chilean sea bass.

If you're seeking a unique dining experience, check out **The Pier at Koredor,** which is perched on a pier over the ocean. The restaurant delivers fresh seafood and a choice of Caribbean-inspired dishes. The view of the ocean is truly stunning and adds to the complete dining experience.

For those preferring a premium eating experience, there's **Restaurant BijBlauw**, located in the historic Pietermaai district. The restaurant delivers a blend of international and local cuisine with a focus on fresh seafood. The menu offers foods such as lobster bisque and pan-seared fish.

Finally, there's **Karakter Curaçao**, which gives a seaside eating experience with great ocean views. The restaurant features a menu of international cuisine and boasts a selection of fresh seafood dishes, as well as vegetarian and gluten-free options.

No matter what your taste buds want, Curaçao has a wealth of great dining selections to fit every palette.

Casual Dining

Casual dining alternatives abound, with everything from local fishing shacks to international brand cafes. Here are some recommendations for casual dining in Curaçao:

Fishalicious: This fish restaurant located in Punda serves clients some of the best seafood on the island. The menu provides a selection of fish dinners, as well as vegetarian alternatives.

El Gaucho: This Argentinian steakhouse located in the heart of Willemstad is famous for its excellent steaks and vast wine selection.

Koko's Beach: This beachside restaurant on the west coast of the island is the perfect location for a relaxing meal or dinner. The menu comprises a range of international dishes, as well as local specialities.

De Visserij: This seafood restaurant is located in the historic Pietermaai area and gives a unique dining experience. Guests may choose their own fish from the on-site fish market and have it prepared to their satisfaction.

Plasa Bieu: This little market in Punda is the excellent backdrop for a leisurely dinner. Here you may acquire a variety of local cuisine, such as stoba (stew), funchi (polenta-like dish), and kabritu (goat meat).

No matter where you go in Curaçao, you're certain to have a delicious meal.

Vegetarian and Vegan Options

Curaçao is a destination that gives a broad array of gourmet possibilities, including options for vegetarians and vegans. Whether you're seeking for a gourmet dining experience or something more informal, you'll find dozens of selections that suit your dietary demands.

One popular location for vegetarian and vegan cuisine is the restaurant titled "**Burgers & More**" in Willemstad, which delivers a selection of delectable **plant-based burgers, sandwiches, and salads.** Another wonderful choice is "**The Green House**," located in Scharloo, which serves a selection of vegetarian and vegan meals made from fresh, locally sourced ingredients.

If you're seeking for foreign cuisine with vegetarian and vegan choices, check out "**Plasa Bieu**" in downtown Willemstad. This open-air market gives a range of Caribbean and Latin American cuisine, many of which are vegetarian or vegan.

For a great eating experience, visit **"BijBlauw,"** which has a unique vegetarian and vegan cuisine with meals that combine Caribbean and world flavors. **"Kome"** in Punda is well worth a visit, as it offers a varied menu including vegetarian and vegan choices that change seasonally.

Curaçao Liqueurs and Cocktails

Curaçao is famous for its unique blue liquor created from the laraha citrus fruit, but there are many other types of liqueurs and cocktails that can be obtained on the island. These drinks often blend local ingredients and flavors to generate unique and delicious beverages.

One notable liqueur is the **Ponche Crema**, a creamy and sweet liqueur produced from eggs, condensed milk, and rum. It is often served as a dessert drink during the holidays but may be enjoyed year-round. Another local delicacy is the **Bolo di Rum**, a rum cake prepared with dried fruit and spices soaked in rum. It is a delicious sweet treat to enjoy with a cup of coffee or tea.

When it comes to cocktails, the **Blue Curaçao** cocktail is a classic. Made with Blue Curaçao, vodka, and orange juice, it is a delightful and vibrant cocktail that is perfect for sipping on the beach. Another famous cocktail is the **Chichi Pisco,** produced with pisco, lime juice, honey, and indigenous herbs.

Visitors may also sample local beer, such as the **Amstel Bright**, a light and pleasant beer that is suited for the island's mild weather. Or, for those who prefer non-alcoholic drinks, there is the refreshing and delectable **Batido**, a fruit shake combined with milk, ice, and local fruit such as papaya, mango, or pineapple.

Whether you enjoy sweet and creamy liqueurs, refreshing cocktails, or local brews, there is something for everyone to appreciate when it comes to Curaçao's drinks and cocktails.

Local Markets and Food Hubs

If you want to explore the local culinary culture, visiting the local markets and food centers is a must. Here are some of the great sites to check out:

Floating Market

The Floating Market in Curaçao is a unique and beautiful spectacle that every traveler should witness. The market is located in the center of Willemstad and features colorful boats from Venezuela, providing a choice of fresh vegetables, seafood, and other local things.

The market has been operating for nearly a century and is a vital component of Curaçao's cultural tradition. Visitors may browse the market, enjoy the fresh fruits and vegetables, and mingle with the friendly vendors who are always happy to share their stories and traditions.

The Floating Market is a must-see destination for everyone who desires to immerse themselves in the unique culture of Curaçao. It's a good opportunity to view the hustle and bustle of the market and see a snapshot of daily life in the Caribbean. Make sure to bring your camera to capture the vivid colors and unique mood of the Floating Market.

Plasa Bieu

Plasa Bieu, also known as **Marshe Bieu,** is a renowned food market in Willemstad, Curaçao, that is recognized for serving up delicious local cuisine. Located in the middle of the city, this busy marketplace features a selection of food stalls and traders providing everything from seafood to stews to snacks.

One of the attractions of Plasa Bieu is the ability to sample real **Krioyo cuisine**, which is a blend of African, European, and Caribbean flavors. Popular foods include stoba (stew), keshi yena (stuffed cheese), and funchi (cornmeal porridge).

The atmosphere at Plasa Bieu is lively and bustling, with locals and tourists both interacting and enjoying the food. It's an excellent area to have a quick bite to eat, or to remain and enjoy a leisurely dinner while soaking up the vibrant ambiance of Willemstad.

If you're a foodie or just wanting to experience the local culture, a visit to Plasa Bieu is a must. Be prepared to arrive hungry and ready to experience some of the finest food that Curaçao has to offer!

Marshe Nobo

Marshe Nobo, also known as the New Market, is a popular site for residents and visitors alike to purchase fresh fruit, seafood, and souvenirs. Located in the center of Willemstad, this busy market is a dynamic hive of activity where tourists can experience the real sights, sounds, and smells of Curaçao.

At Marshe Nobo, you may get everything from exotic fruits and vegetables to locally caught fish and shellfish. The market also has a variety of food kiosks offering traditional meals such as stobá, a substantial stew cooked with goat or beef, and funchi, a cornmeal porridge akin to polenta.

Aside from the fresh food and local cuisine, Marshe Nobo is also noted for its **handcrafted crafts and souvenirs.** Visitors may peruse the booths for unusual goods such as hand-carved wooden figures, vivid paintings, and beaded jewelry.

Whether you want to enjoy the local food, pick up some fresh fruit, or browse for one-of-a-kind souvenirs, Marshe Nobo is a must-visit place in Curaçao. Don't forget to bring your camera and immerse yourself in the vivid culture of this busy market.

Culinary Tours and Experiences

If you're a foodie, then Curaçao has a lot for you! One of the greatest methods to learn the local cuisine and experience it like a true native is by joining a culinary tour or excursion. Here are some excellent possibilities for gastronomic tours and activities in Curaçao:

Flavors of Curaçao Food Tour: This 4-hour walking tour takes you through the streets of Willemstad to experience native cuisine and drinks, including street food, snacks, and traditional dinners. Along the excursion, you'll learn about the history and culture of the island.

Curaçao Liquor & Food Tasting excursion: This trip brings you to some of the island's top distilleries and breweries to try local liquors and beers. You'll also get to consume some traditional foods and cuisines along the trip.

Caribbean Cooking Class: Learn how to create traditional Caribbean cuisine with a local chef in a small-group atmosphere. You'll have hands-on experience making delicacies such as plantains, fish stew, and coconut rice.

Willemstad delicacies and Culture Walking excursion: This 3-hour walk takes you through the historic area of Willemstad to enjoy local specialties and learn about the history and culture of the island. You'll visit local markets, shops, and restaurants to taste a selection of cuisines.

Flavors of the Dutch Caribbean: This food tour takes you on a gourmet excursion through the Dutch Caribbean, with stops in Curaçao, Aruba, and Bonaire. You'll sample local food and drinks, learn about the history and culture of each island, and explore the local markets and businesses.

No matter the excursion or activity you chose, you're assured to have a delightful and amazing time savoring the gastronomic joys of Curaçao!

Cooking Classes and Workshops

Curaçao is an excellent spot for food aficionados who desire to learn how to prepare local dishes and discover the island's particular culinary culture. There are several culinary courses and seminars provided on the island, ranging from indigenous Krioyo cuisine to international fusion specialties.

One popular course for culinary training is at **Landhuis Klein Santa Martha**, a charming historic plantation estate that has been transformed into a cooking school. Here, travelers may learn how to produce traditional Curaçao an dishes such as Keshi Yena and Arepa di Pampuna, as well as other Caribbean and Latin American favorites.

Another choice is the Cooking Class at **Coral Estate**, where you will learn to create a variety of local and international cuisine employing fresh items from the island's gardens and local markets. The program includes a tour of the estate's organic garden, followed by hands-on cooking instruction and a sumptuous meal.

For those interested in vegan and vegetarian cuisine, check out the classes at **Plantiful**, a plant-based café and juice bar that also provides cooking workshops. You may learn how to create healthful and delectable vegan cuisine such as **smoothie bowls, plant-based burgers, and raw desserts.**

If you're interested in a more extensive culinary experience, consider a cooking retreat with **Eat.Drink.Dive**. This company offers a selection of food and drink-themed excursions on the island, including hands-on cooking courses, farm-to-table dining experiences, and tours to local markets and food producers.

No matter what your gastronomic tastes may be, there's a lot for you in Curaçao.

Chocolate Making Workshop

Chocolate connoisseurs visiting Curaçao may enjoy a unique and delectable experience by enrolling in a chocolate-making course. These seminars provide attendees the opportunity to learn about the history and manufacture of chocolate, as well as to produce their own tasty pleasures to take home.

During the lesson, participants will learn about the process of chocolate making, from roasting the cocoa beans to grinding and tempering the chocolate. They will also learn about the numerous sorts of chocolate and the best strategies to employ them in meals.

After the presentation, attendees will have the chance to construct their own chocolates by choosing their favorite flavorings and mix-ins, such as nuts, fruit, and spices. They will also learn how to mold and shape the chocolates before they are set in the refrigerator.

At the completion of the session, participants will get to take home their own handmade chocolates as well as the knowledge and skills they have received throughout the program. These seminars are a fun and delectable way to spend a day in Curaçao, and are appropriate for chocolate enthusiasts of all ages.

Farm Tours & Agrotourism

Curaçao may be a little island, but it is abundant with countryside and local farms that supply fresh, organic food. Farm tours and agrotourism are growing increasingly popular, allowing travelers to view the countryside, get hands-on with farm operations, and learn about local cuisine.

One popular farm excursion is the **Kunuku Aqua Resort**, which includes a tour of their sustainable farm and aquaponics system. Visitors may learn about the different fruits and vegetables growing on the farm, and even help with the harvesting process. The excursion also includes a visit to the aquaponics system, where visitors can observe how fish and plants are grown together in a symbiotic environment.

Another popular agrotourism activity is the Ostrich Farm, which is home to over 600 ostriches. Visitors may take a guided tour of the farm, learn about ostrich behavior and breeding, and even feed the birds. The farm also offers a gift shop providing ostrich commodities such as feathers, eggs, and meat.

For a more immersive experience, guests may book a stay at one of the various agrotourism hotels available on the island. These accommodations provide the possibility to live and work on a farm, learning about sustainable agriculture and organic agricultural processes.

Curaçao's agrotourism business is not only a good chance for travelers to experience local culture, but it also supports the island's economy and helps to foster sustainable farming methods.

Dining Etiquette in Curaçao

Dining etiquette in Curaçao is identical to many other countries. However, here are some key factors to take in mind when dining in Curaçao:

Dress code: In Curaçao, most restaurants have a casual dress code, however some may have severe attire restrictions. It is usually good to check ahead of time.

Tipping: Tipping is popular in Curaçao, and the standard amount is around 10-15% of the overall cost. However, some restaurants may include a service charge, so be sure to check the bill before tipping.

Table manners: When dining in Curaçao, it is considered acceptable to wait for everyone to be served before commencing to eat. It is also normal to use utensils while eating, and to keep your elbows off the table.

Respect local customs: Curaçao is a diversified island with a rich cultural heritage. It is generally recommended to obey local customs and traditions while dining out. For example, some restaurants may not sell pork due to religious considerations.

Be punctual: In Curaçao, it is considered rude to be late for a dinner engagement. If you are running late, it is always best to phone the restaurant and tell them.

By following these straightforward dining etiquette norms, you will secure a great and respectful meal experience in Curaçao.

Best Bars and Nightlife Spots

Curaçao is a vibrant and exciting area, especially when it comes to its nightlife. From sophisticated cocktail bars to beach lounges and live music venues, there are lots of options to choose from. Here are some of the top bars and nightlife locations in Curaçao:

Wet & Wild Beach Club - Located on Mambo Beach Boulevard, Wet & Wild is a popular location for both locals and tourists. It boasts a gorgeous coastal backdrop and contains a wide drink menu, live music, and DJs.

Miles Jazz Cafe - If you're a jazz enthusiast, then you won't want to miss Miles Jazz Cafe. This modest tavern is located in the middle of Willemstad and features live jazz music every night, along with a superb choice of wines and drinks.

Saint Tropez Ocean Club - Situated on Jan Thiel Beach, Saint Tropez is a classy beach club that features excellent ocean views, an extensive beverage menu, and live music on the weekends.

Omundo - Located in the famous Pietermaai area, Omundo is a sophisticated lounge that serves up superb beverages and tapas. It also includes live music on various nights.

Rif Fort Babor - This historic fort has been transformed into a modern shopping and dining complex, and is home to many restaurants and nightlife establishments. The outdoor terrace is a lovely location to grab a drink.

Madero Ocean Club - Situated on the pier of the iconic Mambo Beach Boulevard, Madero gives a quiet beach environment during the day and changes into a lively nightlife at night.

Emporio - This chic bar is located in the midst of Punda and features a sophisticated setting, imaginative beverages, and a superb variety of wines.

27 Curaçao - Located in the upscale Scharloo district, 27 Curaçao is a popular spot for cocktails and nibbles. It includes an outdoor terrace and is famous for its distinctive drink menu.

Curaçao boasts a broad assortment of bars and nightlife establishments that cater to all interests and inclinations. Whether you're hunting for a beach lounge or a stylish cocktail bar, you're sure to find something that suits your style in Curaçao.

Nightlife Etiquette

When it comes to nightlife etiquette in Curaçao, there are a few things to keep in mind:

Dress Code: Most nightclubs in Curaçao have a dress code, so it's important to dress appropriately. For men, a collared shirt and dress shoes are usually required. Women should avoid wearing flip-flops or beachwear.

Respect: It's important to respect other club-goers and the staff. Avoid being overly aggressive or disrespectful, and don't try to start fights or arguments.

Drink Responsibly: While it's okay to have a good time, it's important to drink responsibly. Pace yourself, and don't overindulge. Always have a designated driver or plan for a safe ride home.

Be Aware of Your Surroundings: Keep an eye on your personal belongings and be aware of your surroundings. Stay away from questionable areas and don't go out alone if possible.

Have Fun: Most importantly, have fun and enjoy yourself! Curaçao has a vibrant nightlife scene, and there's something for everyone, so let loose and make some memories.

CHAPTER 9: EVENTS AND FESTIVALS IN CURAÇAO

Curaçao is a lively and varied island that is home to a spectrum of many cultures and nations. As such, the island plays host to a range of intriguing events and festivals throughout the year, each presenting a unique insight into local traditions and customs. Whether you're interested in music, food, or art, there is sure to be an event or celebration that suits your interests.

Major Celebrations and Holidays

Here are some of the significant celebrations and holidays to look out for when visiting Curaçao:

Carnival:

Curaçao Carnival is one of the biggest and most popular celebrations in the country. It is a brilliant and colorful event that takes place **every year before the start of Lent**. The carnival is a time of celebration, with music, dancing, parades, and a general sense of joy and happiness.

The carnival season in Curaçao officially starts on **January 6**, which is known as Dia di Reis, or Three Kings Day. From this day onward, the island is jammed with several carnival-related events, including costume contests, street festivities, and live music performances. The principal element of the carnival is the Grand Parade, which takes place on the Sunday before Ash Wednesday. During the parade, you can expect to see wonderfully designed floats, bright costumes, and plenty of dancing and music.

One of the most recognized features of Curaçao Carnival is the **Tumba music**. This is a unique style of music that mixes African, Latin, and Caribbean rhythms, and is played throughout the carnival season. The Tumba music is a vital component of the carnival, and you can expect to hear it anywhere you go at this time of year.

Another key highlight of Curaçao Carnival is the gastronomy. Many local restaurants and street vendors provide a choice of superb meals and drinks throughout the carnival season, including traditional specialities like **Keshi Yena and fish stews, as well as refreshing cocktails and beer**.

If you're hoping to visit Curaçao during the carnival season, be sure to book your accommodation and tickets well in advance, as this is a particularly popular time to come. And don't forget to pack your dancing shoes, as you won't be able to resist the enticing sounds of Curaçao Carnival.

<u>Dia di San Juan:</u>

Dia di San Juan is a notable celebration observed in Curaçao every year on **June 24th**. The holiday is also known as Saint John's Day and is commemorated to honor the birth of Saint John the Baptist. This festival is conducted all throughout the world, but the celebration in Curaçao has its own distinct flavor.

The rituals begin with a traditional Catholic service at daybreak, followed by a procession when people carry a statue of Saint John the Baptist through the streets. The procession is accompanied by music, dancing, and traditional drums. After the procession, the statue is taken back to the church, where it is adorned with flowers.

As the day unfolds, the festivities continue with music, dancing, and food. People dress up in colorful costumes and perform the traditional tambu and salsa dances. There are also food sellers providing traditional meals such as arepa di pampuna, a wonderful pumpkin pancake, and sopa di mondongo, a tripe soup. The celebration culminates with a magnificent fireworks finale at midnight.

Dia di San Juan is a celebration of Curaçao's rich cultural past, and is a must-see for everyone visiting the island. The festival is a terrific opportunity to discover the island's unique blend of African, European, and Caribbean traditions, and is a genuine feast for the senses.

The Seú Harvest Festival is a traditional celebration that takes place in Curaçao each year, often in the month of May. The festival is an important cultural event that is profoundly rooted in the island's history and customs.

Curaçao International Dive Festival

The Curaçao International Dive Festival is an annual event that unites divers from around the world to see the stunning underwater environment surrounding the island. The festival is a celebration of Curaçao's rich marine life, coral reefs, and shipwrecks, and includes a range of activities and events for divers of all skills.

During the festival, divers may take part in a choice of guided dives and lectures arranged by local dive companies and professionals. The event also involves a picture and video contest, where divers may showcase their underwater photography and filmmaking expertise. In addition, there are various social events, including beach parties and live music performances.

The event is generally held in **September or October** and is a superb occasion for divers to explore the crystal-clear waters of Curaçao, make new friends, and celebrate their love of diving. Whether you're a seasoned diver or a rookie, the Curaçao International Dive Festival is an event not to be missed.

<u>Curaçao Pride</u>

Curaçao Pride is an annual celebration of the LGBTQ+ community in Curaçao. It generally takes place in **late September** and encompasses a multitude of events such as festivities, parades, and cultural activities. The event provides an opportunity for the community to come together to celebrate diversity and inclusivity in Curaçao.

The focus of Curaçao Pride is the colorful parade which goes through the streets of Willemstad, displaying the life and creativity of the LGBTQ+ community. Participants dress up in amazing costumes, wave rainbow flags, and dance to joyous music as they make their way throughout the city.

In addition to the parade, there are also a variety of events and cultural activities throughout the week-long festival. These include dance parties, drag performances, art exhibitions, and film screenings, among others.

Curaçao Pride is not merely a celebration of the LGBTQ+ population, but also a reflection of the island's devotion to tolerance and diversity. It is a time when locals and visitors alike may get together to celebrate love and acceptance in a safe and pleasant setting.

Seú Harvest Festival

The Seú Harvest Festival is a time to celebrate the completion of the harvest season, and to show thankfulness for the plenty that the land has given. It is a time when people join together to share food, music, and dancing, and to enjoy the company of friends and family.

One of the most crucial components of the Seú Harvest Festival is the music. The event is famous for its vivid and powerful rhythms, which are played on indigenous instruments such as the tambú, the wiri, and the chapi. The music is complemented by vivid clothes and frenzied dancing, and the attitude is one of joy and celebration.

In addition to the music and dancing, the Seú Harvest Festival also features a selection of traditional dishes and drinks, including local delicacies such as karni stoba (beef stew), funchi (cornmeal mush), and kadushi (cactus soup). Visitors to the event may also taste a choice of native drinks, including the island's legendary Blue Curaçao liqueur.

Whether you are a local resident or a visitor to the island, the festival is an opportunity to appreciate the peculiar traditions and customs of this beautiful and lively community.

Christmas and New Year's Eve:

Christmas in Curaçao is a joyous and lovely time of the year. The Christmas season is celebrated with a unique blend of local customs and international standards. From mid-November to early January, the island is decorated with dazzling lights, and the air is filled with the sounds of cheerful tunes.

One of the most noteworthy traditions is the lighting of the Christmas tree, which takes place at the historic Brion Square in downtown Willemstad. The tree is adorned with brilliant lights and decorations, and a grand ceremony is planned to mark its ceremonial lighting. Locals and tourists converge to enjoy the Christmas ambiance and take pictures with the brilliantly adorned tree.

Another habit is the **singing of Aguinaldos**, which are traditional Christmas songs. These songs are sung in Papiamentu, the local language, and illustrate the island's cultural richness. Some popular Aguinaldos include **"Pasku ta Llegando" and "Dulce Navidad."**

During the Christmas season, many restaurants and hotels provide unique seasonal menus and events. Visitors may enjoy a choice of traditional and international dishes, as well as live music and entertainment.

On Christmas Day, families assemble to enjoy a feast of delicious food and spend time with loved ones. Some popular delicacies include **Ayaka**, a traditional dish cooked with meat and cornmeal wrapped in banana leaves, and Stoba di Kabritu, a stew made with goat meat.

The holiday season finishes with **New Year's Eve celebrations,** which are known for their breathtaking fireworks displays. Locals and tourists converge on the beaches or in the city to welcome the new year with pleasure and optimism.

New Year's Eve is a big occasion in Curaçao, just as in many other parts of the world. There are many festivals, celebrations, and fireworks displays happening over the island.

One notable spot for New Year's Eve is the **Queen Emma Bridge** in Willemstad, where people meet to enjoy the fireworks display over the sea. The bridge affords a beautiful view of the fireworks, and it is also a vibrant and joyful spot to be.

Many hotels, restaurants, and bars also conduct special events and festivities for New Year's Eve. These events often incorporate live music, DJs, food, drinks, and of course, champagne to bring in the new year. Some of the most popular sites for New Year's Eve celebrations include the **Renaissance Curaçao Resort & Casino, the Avila Beach Hotel, and the Santa Barbara Beach & Golf Resort.**

It's vital to note that many companies require reservations for their New Year's Eve events, so be sure to plan early if you want to attend a specific party or celebration. Additionally, it's always a good idea to prepare for transportation in advance, as taxis and other transit services can be in considerable demand on New Year's Eve.

Arts and Musical Festivals

Curaçao North Sea Jazz Festival:

The Curaçao North Sea Jazz Festival is one of the largest and most popular jazz events in the Caribbean. This **three-day festival** offers a variety of world-renowned artists from numerous genres, including jazz, R&B, soul, and pop.

The festival takes place annually in **late August** at the World Trade Center Piscadera Bay in Willemstad, the capital city of Curaçao. The area features numerous stages, food and drink vendors, and plenty of space for festival-goers to relax and enjoy the music.

Past performances at the Curaçao North Sea Jazz Festival have included notable artists such as **Stevie Wonder, Lionel Richie, Alicia Keys, John Legend, Bruno Mars,** and many more. In addition to the major stage activities, the festival also provides smaller intimate concerts, meet-and-greet sessions with artists, and after-parties.

Tickets for the event are generally available for purchase several months in advance, and may be obtained online or through specific local retailers. It's suggested to buy tickets early, because the event normally sells out swiftly.

If you're a music aficionado visiting Curaçao, the North Sea Jazz Festival is surely an event not to be missed. With a terrific list of performers, a magnificent setting, and a joyous and festive atmosphere, this festival is certain to be an unforgettable event.

Dia di Rincon:

Dia di Rincon is a lively and colorful celebration that takes place in the modest village of **Rincon**, located in the **northwest region of Curaçao**. Celebrated every year on **April 30th**, the event is a celebration of the island's cultural heritage, music, and traditions. The festival is a showcase of local folklore, arts & crafts, traditional music, and dancing.

During the festival, the streets of Rincon are filled with dazzling colors and sounds, with people dressed in traditional costumes and dancing to the beat of tambu music. The tambu music is a traditional Afro-Caribbean music genre that evolved in Curaçao during the days of slavery. The rhythm of tambu is generated by a group of drummers playing traditional instruments built from oil barrels and goat leather.

Dia di Rincon is an opportunity to learn the particular culture of Curaçao, to eat local food, and to purchase homemade goods and souvenirs. The event attracts people from all over the world, who come to enjoy the music, dance, and food, and to immerse themselves in the island's rich cultural past.

The celebration has its beginnings in the Catholic habit of commemorating saints, notably the remembrance of Rincon's patron saint, San Juan Bautista. The festival has turned into a cultural event that emphasizes the diversity of the island's residents and its history.

Visitors to the Dia di Rincon event are asked to honor local customs and traditions, to dress appropriately, and to engage in the celebrations with respect and openness. The festival is a time for people to come together and enjoy the rich cultural heritage of Curaçao, and to respect the island's history and traditions.

Curaçao International BlueSeas Event

The Curaçao International BlueSeas event is an annual music festival hosted in Willemstad, Curaçao. This **three-day event is** a celebration of local and international music, featuring some of the greatest artists from throughout the world.

The festival takes place in **September** and encompasses a range of music genres, including blues, jazz, reggae, soul, and funk. The event is done at several venues over the island, with enormous stages built up in notable spots such the Renaissance Mall and Riffort Village.

In addition to the live music performances, the festival also provides workshops and masterclasses with notable performers, allowing an opportunity for aspiring musicians to learn from the greatest in the industry.

The Curaçao International BlueSeas Festival is a cultural and musical extravaganza, welcoming travelers from all over the world to experience the island's active music culture. Whether you're a music aficionado or just hunting for a fun and unusual event, this festival is not to be missed.

Curaçao International Film Festival

The Curaçao International Film Festival, popularly known as CIFF, is an annual film festival held in the city of Willemstad, Curaçao. The festival includes a mix of international films, with a focus on Caribbean and Latin American cinema.

The festival was founded in 2012 and has since become one of the most renowned movie events in the region. The festival generally takes place over the course of **several days** and contains a combination of film screenings, workshops, and special events.

CIFF aspires to promote cultural diversity and social awareness through cinema, bringing together artists, industry professionals, and film fans from around the world. The festival gives a place for budding talent and established filmmakers to exhibit their work and communicate with audiences.

In addition to film screenings, the festival also features a number of additional events, including Q&A sessions with filmmakers, panel discussions, and networking opportunities. The festival also includes educational sessions for budding filmmakers and students interested in film production.

Whether you are a seasoned film aficionado or just seeking to explore the world of cinema, the Curaçao International Film Festival is not to be missed.

Tumba Festival

The Tumba Festival is an annual event that is conducted during the Carnival season in Curaçao. The festival commemorates the island's vibrant music culture and is an important cultural event in the country.

Tumba is a genre of music that evolved in Curaçao and is defined by its fast-paced beat and joyous melodies. The festival features a series of activities where local artists compete to create the greatest Tumba song of the year. The competitions are held in several categories, including best lyrics, best music, and best performance.

The Tumba Festival is not just about music, but there are also amazing parades and colorful costumes on show during the Carnival season. The event is a celebration of Curaçao an culture and tradition, and guests can expect to be immersed in the vibrant and joyous setting.

Whether you are a music aficionado, a cultural enthusiast, or simply hunting for a good time, the Tumba Festival is a must-see event in Curaçao.

CHAPTER 10: SHOPPING AND SOUVENIRS

Shopping in Curaçao is more than simply purchasing trinkets, it's a cultural trip. The bustling markets, local crafts, and unique items are an invitation to discover the island's rich history and culture.

Local Crafts and Artwork

Here are some ideas on the top local crafts and artwork to look out for:

Chichi Sculptures - These colorful and eccentric sculptures are a symbol of the island's past and are constructed by local craftsmen. They come in many sizes and patterns, making them a perfect souvenir to take home.

Handmade Jewelry - Curaçao is home to numerous superb jewelers who manufacture exquisite things with local materials such as seashells, coral, and semi-precious stones. These one-of-a-kind sculptures make for wonderful gifts or a unique treat for yourself.

Artisanal Paintings - Curaçao's beautiful colors and sceneries have inspired numerous local artists, who produce magnificent paintings portraying the island's beauty, people, and history. Look out for artwork by local artists in galleries and markets around the island.

Local Textiles - From colorful woven carpets and hammocks to hand-embroidered tablecloths and napkins, Curaçao has a rich tradition of textile creation. These handmade things make for wonderful gifts and are a unique way to bring a bit of the island's culture to your residence.

Local Food and Drink - Curaçao's cuisine is a combination of Dutch, Caribbean, and Latin American tastes, and native food and drink goods like hot sauce, rum, and coffee make for wonderful souvenirs to take home and enjoy with friends and family. Look out for locally created versions of these foods in markets and specialist food stores across the island.

When shopping for local crafts and artwork in Curaçao, be sure to support local artisans and buy directly from them wherever practicable. This not only confirms that you are acquiring a genuine, high-quality product but also helps to support the local economy and sustain the island's distinct cultural tradition.

Unique Souvenirs and Gifts

Here are some interesting souvenir and gift ideas to take home with you:

Curaçao Liqueur: One of the most popular souvenirs to take home from Curaçao is a bottle of the famed Curaçao Liqueur. The brilliant blue tint is a trademark of the island and may be found in numerous flavors such as orange, lemon, and tamarind.

Handmade Crafts: There are many local artists and artisans on the island that make unique goods such as pottery, handwoven baskets, and jewelry. These are great gifts and souvenirs that reflect the island's originality and artistic flare.

Aloe Vera items: Curaçao is home to several aloe vera plants, and goods derived from the plant are widely available on the island. These comprise creams, lotions, and other skincare things that make excellent gifts for anyone hunting for a little bit of island-style pampering.

Dutch Cheese: Curaçao has a considerable Dutch influence, and as such, travelers may find a choice of Dutch cheeses on the island. These are fantastic gifts for cheese lovers back home.

Local Spices and Sauces: Curaçao's cuisine is famous for its bold flavors, and travelers may bring a taste of the island home with them by purchasing native spices and sauces. These include hot sauces, jerk spice, and other Caribbean-inspired combinations.

T-Shirts & Beachwear: No visit to Curaçao is complete without a day at the beach, and travelers may buy a choice of beachwear, including bikinis, cover-ups, and hats. T-shirts and other clothing goods with the Curaçao flag or other island-inspired designs are wonderful gifts for friends and family back home.

Whether you're shopping for a gift to bring back for a loved one or a unique keepsake to remind you of your holiday, there are plenty of possibilities to choose from in Curaçao.

Best Shopping Areas and Markets

Here are some of the main shopping areas and marketplaces in Curaçao:

Renaissance Mall: Located in the core of Willemstad, Renaissance Mall is a shopper's paradise. The mall is home to more than 50 high-end shops, including luxury brands such as Louis Vuitton, Michael Kors, and Gucci.

Punda: This historic sector in Willemstad is a must-visit for shopping aficionados. The colorful houses and small streets are home to diverse boutiques providing everything from souvenirs to local crafts and artwork.

Otrobanda: Located across the Sint Anna Bay from Punda, Otrobanda is another excellent shopping center. The district is home to a mix of local and international merchants, as well as the famed Marshe Nobo market.

Promenade Shopping Center: This open-air mall is located in the upscale district of Pietermaai and gives a unique shopping experience. The mall has a mix of local and international stores, as well as restaurants and cafés.

Floating Market: The Floating Market is a unique shopping experience that shouldn't be missed. Boats from neighboring Venezuela arrive along the coast at Willemstad, delivering fresh fruit and seafood.

Plasa Bieu: This busy food market is also a good spot to find local arts and crafts. The market is home to many vendors providing everything from locally-made hot sauce to hand-woven baskets.

Landhuis Bloemhof: This historic plantation palace is today home to an art gallery and souvenir shop. Visitors may examine a vast assortment of locally-made crafts, jewelry, and artwork.

No matter what you're seeking for, Curaçao delivers something for every customer. So, be sure to visit these shopping shops and markets on your next holiday to Curaçao.

How To Save Money While Shopping in Curaçao

Curaçao is a wonderful region to purchase for souvenirs, gifts, and native handicrafts. However, it's vital to know how to save money while shopping in Curaçao. Here are some ideas to help you make the most of your shopping budget:

Shop at Local Markets: One of the simplest techniques to save money while shopping in Curaçao is to visit the local markets. These markets feature a large selection of local products and handicrafts, and prices are often less than in tourist zones. Some of the notable markets in Curaçao include the Willemstad Market, Floating Market, and Marshe Nobo.

Check Prices: Before making a purchase, take some time to check prices at several retailers. Often, prices could vary drastically, and you might buy the similar item at a cheaper price elsewhere.

Look for Discounts and offers: Many shops in Curaçao provide discounts and special deals, especially during the off-season. Keep an eye out for signs and promotions while you're shopping.

Buy Duty-Free: If you're heading beyond the European Union, you may take advantage of the duty-free shopping in Curaçao. This may save you a considerable lot of money on luxury products, such as jewelry and designer garments.

Bargain: Bargaining is popular in Curaçao, notably at marketplaces and souvenir businesses. Don't be reluctant to haggle the price, and you may be able to acquire a better deal.

By following these advice, you will save money while shopping in Curaçao and still bring back unique souvenirs and gifts.

Tips For Bargaining And Negotiating

Bargaining while buying in Curaçao may be a wonderful experience, but it's vital to know the local standards and etiquette. Here are some recommendations to assist you acquire the finest deals while shopping:

Start with a smile: Greet the merchant or vendor with a smile and be pleasant. A friendly attitude may go a long way in developing a relationship and setting a good tone for the bargaining process.

Do your research: Before you start haggling, make sure you know the normal price of the item you want to acquire. This will offer you a framework for negotiating and protect you from overpaying.

Don't be afraid to walk away: If the vendor is not ready to bargain or is asking for a price that is too high, don't be afraid to walk away. Sometimes, moving away could help you secure a better offer.

Make a counteroffer: When the merchant gives you a price, make a counteroffer that is lower than what they are asking for. You may then bargain back and forth until you find a price that works for both of you.

Bundle products: If you are buying numerous goods from the same supplier, strive to bundle them together and negotiate a better price for the bundle.

Remain courteous: Remember to remain polite throughout the bargaining process. Don't be harsh or combative, and try to have a nice attitude. After all, bargaining is designed to be a happy and participatory activity.

By following these tips, you will save money while shopping in Curaçao and have a good time bargaining and negotiating with the locals.

How To Shop Tax Free and Get Shopping Refund

If you're thinking of purchasing in Curaçao, it's worth mentioning that you may take advantage of the tax-free shopping system. To qualify for tax-free shopping, you need to be a non-resident of Curaçao and have spent a minimum of **ANG 50 (or the equivalent in another currency)** on **eligible items** at a **single retailer** on the **same day.**

Here's how the tax-free purchase method works:

Look for stores that give tax-free shopping: Not all stores in Curaçao participate in the tax-free shopping program, therefore search for signs that indicate the store provides tax-free shopping.

Make your purchase: Once you've picked whatever you desire to buy, make your transaction and preserve your receipt.

Request a tax-free form: Ask the store to give you a tax-free form, which you'll need to fill out with your personal data and passport number.

Get your form stamped: Before leaving Curaçao, take your tax-free form to the airport or cruise terminal and present it, along with your **receipts and passport**, at the tax-free return station. The clerk will stamp your documents and provide you a refund.

Note that there is a small fee for tax-free shopping, which is generally roughly **5-7%** of the transaction value. This fee is removed from your tax-free refund.

How To Avoid Crowd While Touring Curaçao

Curaçao is a prominent tourist destination, and its several attractions attract massive crowds, especially during peak holiday season. However, there are ways to avoid the throng and still have a pleasant vacation touring the island.

One technique to avoid crowds is to **visit popular destinations during off-peak hours**. Many travelers prefer to see landmarks in the morning and early afternoon, so consider visiting in the late afternoon or evening when the crowds have gone down.

Another approach to avoid crowds is to **visit lesser-known places.** Curaçao provides countless hidden treasures that are just as beautiful and interesting as the major landmarks, yet they are generally disregarded by tourists. Research these hidden treasures before your trip, and plan to visit them during your stay.

You could also consider taking **private tours or hiring a personal guide**. Private trips could be more pricey, but they give a more tailored experience, and you can avoid the throngs that sometimes come with group tours.

Lastly, if you are staying at a hotel, ask the front desk for advice on less crowded beaches, restaurants, and other activities. They may be able to give insider insights and ideas to help you avoid the crowds and enjoy a more calm and happy time in Curaçao.

CHAPTER 11: TRAVELING WITH DISABILITY

Curaçao is becoming more and more accessible for persons traveling with limitations. While there are still some challenges, there are also thousands of solutions and services available to make your vacation a success.

For instance, some hotels and resorts on the island have been developed or remodeled to accommodate persons with disabilities. From wheelchair ramps and elevators to accessible rooms and bathrooms, you may locate a range of solutions to satisfy your wants. It's essential to phone the hotel or resort ahead of time to discuss your unique needs and make any needed arrangements.

In addition to hotels, there are also several activities and attractions that are accessible to those with disabilities. The island's beaches offer a number of beach wheelchairs available for hiring, and many of the island's attractions have accessible alternatives. For example, the Curaçao Sea Aquarium has wheelchair-friendly pathways across the complex, while the Dolphin Academy offers an assisted swim program for travelers with disabilities.

It's crucial to realize that while Curaçao is becoming more accessible, there may still be some challenges to travel, such as rough terrain or limited accessibility in some regions. It's crucial to do some research and plan ahead to guarantee that your holiday is as enjoyable and delightful as possible.

Here are some key pieces of advice to aid make your trip as simple and joyful as possible:

Plan ahead: Research your holiday possibilities, accessible hotels, and activities in advance. This will give you a clear idea of what to expect and help you to make any essential planning beforehand.

Contact your hotel: Make sure to let your hotel know in advance about any unique accommodations you may need. Many hotels have accessible rooms available, although it's advisable to check ahead to avoid any surprises.

Use a travel agency: Consider working with a travel agent who specializes in accessible travel. They can aid you discover the greatest hotels and activities to match your wants.

Bring your own equipment: If you require any specific equipment, such as a wheelchair or mobility scooter, consider bringing your own. This will assure that you have everything you need and eliminate any issues with rental equipment.

Research transit choices: Check with the local transit authorities to find out about accessible opportunities. Many buses and taxis in Curaçao are geared to assist individuals with disabilities.

Be patient: Be prepared to confront some barriers along the path, such as lack of accessibility to certain places or transportation concerns. It's vital to be patient and adaptive, and to remember that your trip is about the experiences and memories you build.

Curaçao is a destination that welcomes all travelers, including those with disabilities. With the right preparation and resources, you can enjoy all that the island has to offer.

Travel Resources for Disabled Persons

Here are some travel resources that can help:

Accessible Curaçao: Accessible Curaçao is a non-profit organization that gives information and aid for handicapped persons visiting the island. They may help with things like accessible transportation, hotels, and tourist visits.
https://www.accessiblecuracao.com/

Curaçao Accessible Tours: Curaçao Accessible Tours is a tour firm that specializes in giving accessible tours for handicapped individuals. They offer a variety of trips and activities, including beach excursions, cultural tours, and nature walks.
www.curacao-accessible.com

AccessibleTravel.Online:
AccessibleTravel.Online is a website that delivers information on accessible travel sites across the world. They have a section particularly for Curaçao, which offers information on accessible hotels, transportation, and activities. https://accessibletravel.online/

Disabled Travelers: Disabled Travelers is a website that provides travel options for handicapped travelers. They have a section on Curaçao, which provides information about accessible hotels, transportation, and activities.
www.disabledtravelers.com

Special Needs at Sea: Special Needs at Sea is a corporation that provides equipment rentals for disabled passengers, such as scooters, wheelchairs, and portable oxygen tanks. They may deliver the equipment directly to your hotel or cruise ship.
https://www.specialneedsatsea.com/

Curaçao Airport Partners: Curaçao Airport Partners provides help for disabled travelers at the airport, including wheelchair assistance and special transportation services.
https://www.curacao-airport.com/

Caribbean Disabled Sailing Association: The Caribbean Disabled Sailing Association is a non-profit organization that provides sailing opportunities for impaired adults. They give sailing holidays throughout the Caribbean, including Curaçao.
http://caribbeandisabledsailing.com/

When coming to Curaçao with a handicap, it is usually a good idea to study and prepare prior.

Contacting the local tourist board and hotels in advance can aid ensure that your expectations are fulfilled throughout your holiday.

Solo Travel

Curaçao is a generally safe and pleasurable place for lone visitors. The island is famed for its friendly inhabitants, magnificent beaches, and broad array of activities that appeal to a variety of interests. As with any expedition, it is necessary to use common sense and take care to ensure your safety. If you feel uneasy, leave the situation immediately.

When traveling alone in Curaçao, it is advisable to remain in well-lit areas and avoid walking alone at night, especially in secluded regions. Stick to well-trafficked tourist spots and be careful of your surroundings at all times. Avoid hitchhiking and illegal cabs. Always employ official taxis, public transportation, or rental autos from trustworthy sources.

It is also important to alert someone of your trip intentions and location, especially if you desire to wander off the main route. Keep critical papers such as your passport and travel insurance in a secure spot, and consider wearing a money belt or other disguised wallet to keep your things safe.

For lone travelers who are wanting to meet new people, Curaçao gives a range of chances to communicate and connect with other visitors and residents. Consider joining a group tour, visiting a local event or festival, or taking part in a cultural activity or class. Many hotels and hostels also offer social events and activities that may be a good opportunity to meet other travelers.

Lone travelers will enjoy a safe and happy journey in Curaçao with these tips. Remember to always trust your instincts and prioritize your safety.

CHAPTER 12: HELPFUL WEBSITES AND RESOURCES

If you're planning a vacation to Curaçao, there are many useful websites and tools available to help you organize your trip and make the most of your time on the island. Here are a few to get you started:

Curaçao Tourist Board: The official tourist website for Curaçao, including information on attractions, lodgings, eating, events, and more. https://www.curacao.com/

TripAdvisor: A popular website for reviews and suggestions on hotels, restaurants, and activities in Curaçao, as well as forums where you can ask questions and receive advice from other tourists. www.tripadvisor.com

Visit Curaçao: Another website giving information on attractions, activities, lodgings, and events in Curaçao. www.curacao.com

Curaçao Chronicle: A news and information website covering events and developments in Curaçao, including travel-related news and updates. https://curacaochronicle.com/

Curaçao Airport: The official website of Curaçao's airport, offering flight information, airport services, and travel guides.
www.curacao-airport.com

Curaçao Ports Authority: The official website of Curaçao's ports, offering information about cruise ship arrivals and departures, as well as other maritime and freight services.
https://www.curports.com/

By using these websites and resources, you can plan your trip to Curaçao with confidence, knowing that you have access to up-to-date information and advice from professionals and other visitors.

Final Thoughts.

As you prepare to travel to Curaçao, it is necessary to research and plan properly to assure a smooth and happy holiday. Curaçao is a wonderful and diversified island with a rich cultural past, stunning beaches, and a lively nightlife.

Remember to carry adequate clothing and gear for the activities you plan to pursue, and take the vital actions to be safe and healthy while traveling. It is also important to purchase travel insurance to cover any unanticipated complications.

Curaçao is a nice and hospitable destination for all types of people, particularly those with disabilities and solo travelers. With the necessary supplies and planning, you may have a safe and pleasant trip on this magnificent island.

Whether you're seeking adventure, relaxation, or cultural experiences, Curaçao delivers something for everyone. Take the time to explore the island's hidden treasures, eat the traditional food, and participate in the different festivals and events that take place throughout the year.

A holiday to Curaçao promises to be a great experience filled with friendly hospitality, stunning scenery, and exhilarating activities. Happy travels!

Printed in Great Britain
by Amazon

23536979R00159